MW01625494

BOOKS BY ANN DAVISON

Last Voyage

My Ship Is So Small

Home Was an Island

In the Wake of the Gemini

In the Wake of the GEMINI

Top left. A picturesque creek at Sea Island City, New Jersey. *Top right. Gemini* at the Peterborough Lift Lock on the Trent-Severn Waterways, Ontario, Canada. *Bottom left. Gemini* in the tree-tops, waiting to "go down" in the Kirkfield lift lock on the Trent-Severn Waterways, Ontario, Canada. *Bottom right.* The author in the cockpit of the *Gemini.*

ANN DAVISON

In the Wake of the GEMINI

Boston Toronto

LITTLE, BROWN AND COMPANY

LIBRARY OF CONGRESS CATALOG CARD NO. 62–8070

FIRST EDITION

Published simultaneously in Canada
by Little, Brown & Company (Canada) Limited

PRINTED IN THE UNITED STATES OF AMERICA

For Murry Sims, M.D.

Contents

PART I	Atlantic Seaboard	1
PART II	Canals	73
PART III	Lakes	118
PART IV	Rivers	169
PART V	Gulf	239

PART ONE

Atlantic Seaboard

i

"AND what's a pretty gal like you doing all by herself in a boat?" asked the genial lockmaster as I carefully brought the little outboard alongside the rough lock wall.

Being neither young nor beautiful, I was absolutely charmed, of course. Moreover, it was early in the morning and, as anyone knows, a compliment in the morning is worth half a dozen at any other time of day.

These wonderful Americans, I thought, always romanticizing a situation. No fair-haired female in the headlines could be anything but a gorgeous blonde, and if I was murdered overnight my seventeen-foot outboard cruiser would become a luxury yacht. To an American a lone woman is a contradiction in terms, and a lone woman in a boat cannot possibly be left at that. She becomes a pretty gal. And that I like. Especially do I like "gal." "Woman" always conjures up a Ceres-like creature to my mind, a deep-bosomed wench, wide-hipped, who's been at the calories again, and a rather depressing spectacle to anyone with an incipient weight problem. "Girl" once you are not is absurd if not humiliating, but "gal" has a fine swagger to it and you can wear it all your life.

"Where are you going?" asked the lockmaster, busily entering the name and number of my boat on a form.

"Miami."

He looked startled. "Miami, Florida? You're going the wrong way. You're going north. Miami's way down south from here."

"I know," I said, "I'm going by the Great Lakes and the Mississippi River."

"Good grief," he said, "and where have you come from?"

"Miami," I said.

"All the way up from Miami? Why, that must be nearly two thousand miles from here. How did you come — by the Intracoastal to New York?"

I nodded.

"Oh my, that's quite a trip you're making."

"Nearly six thousand miles before I'm through."

"For Pete's sake. Aren't you afraid?"

"What of?"

"Well, supposing an engine breaks down. Can you fix it? What would you do?"

I pointed out that since there were two motors it was highly unlikely they would both break down together, and in the event of the failure of one the other would take me in somewhere.

The lockmaster looked baffled. "Are you advertising something?" he said. "Why are you doing this?" But the valves had been opened and fortunately the roar of the waterfall drowned any further conversation. Although this particular conversation had taken place somewhere pretty nearly every day since I had left home, I had never been able to come up with a satisfactory concise answer as to why I was making the trip. Simply to want to was never enough ("But alone?"). And in point of fact does anyone ever really know exactly why they do anything? I start out with one reason and very often finish with another, having run through several others on the way. Most projects seem to undergo many changes between inception and practice, and frequently end up bearing little resemblance to the original idea. So with my cruise. The actual decision to make it goes back a few years, shortly after I arrived in New York, a wide-eyed new chum from Britain. New York made its usual thundering impact upon a newcomer and what with one thing and another I was consumed with curiosity. It is impossible to ignore the incredible human endeavor behind New York, the extraordinary ambition and vision that raised those towers, or the teeming lives, love and hell that goes on in them. And yet on the whole, people don't get born in New York so much. They go there. Where from, I wondered, and why? I decided someday to take a tour round the country and find out. The time was not then, but the idea settled down in the back of my mind to wait. It reappeared a few years later when I was living in the Bahamas with a boat. Not on a boat. I was living ashore in the normal manner with my boat in the harbor, but we shared a name and had become so identified with one another that people kept getting us mixed up. She was the *Felicity Ann*, the twenty-three-foot sloop in which I had made a singlehanded crossing of the Atlantic Ocean in 1953. The first time, and so far as I know, the only time a woman has done such a thing, and it attracted a certain amount of what the younger newspaper reporters persist in calling notoriety (which intrigues me

— do they really mean it or has the connotation changed again?) and at first after I had made the crossing I was really rather pleased with myself. Nowadays, with all these do-it-yourself psychoanalysis kits in all the popular magazines, I am not so sure. It is, perhaps, a little embarrassing to be caught with so much id showing.

Anyway, there I was in Nassau with this boat and precious little money. I make an absolutely fascinating but precarious living by doing whatever I happen to like doing best at the time — flying an airplane, farming an island, sailing an ocean — and writing about it. When I see bottom through the royalties it is time to think of a new venture, and in Nassau bottom was definitely showing. That is when the dormant idea of making a Stateside tour woke up.

There is usually an overlap in my change of ventures so that they are invariably related to one another in some form. A singular turn of economy (shown nowhere else, I may say) impels me to use some leftover equipment, material or idea, from the previous ploy, which in this case was a boat. So naturally it would be a boat ride, and the maps showed that one could cover about a third of the country by water, starting, say, at Miami and going up to New York, then by the Hudson River and the Erie Canal and Oswego Canal to Lake Ontario, across the Lake to Canada and through the Province of Ontario by the Trent Canal system to Georgian Bay. Thence by the North Channel, Lake Huron and the Mackinac Straits to Lake Michigan and Chicago. From Chicago by the Illinois and Mississippi rivers to the Gulf of Mexico, across the Gulf to the west coast of Florida and back to

Miami. It seemed to offer a fairly representative view of the country and would undoubtedly make a lovely ride, so I started to fit out the *Felicity Ann* with great enthusiasm but no regard for the fact that if I had set out to do so I could have hardly devised a more unsuitable craft for the voyage ahead.

Fitting-out is a procedure in which the hull of a vessel, her masts, rigging (all those wires and ropes that hold things up, down or tight), the engine, and/or sails are gone over lynx-eyed, and renewed, patched or repaired until the ship is ready to go to sea prepared for the worst. For cruising vessels under sail or power it is an annual event at least, and certainly one to be undergone before embarking on a voyage of any length; and it is invariably more costly, involved and long drawn out than is ever allowed for at the onset.

The fitting-out of the *Felicity Ann* for the Grand Tour was no exception, but the usual interminable delays gave me time to look more searchingly into the venture and face the irrefutable fact that I was preparing the wrong boat for the job. *Felicity Ann* was essentially a deep-sea sailing vessel, but on the forthcoming trip there would be very little deep water and very little opportunity for sailing. Much of the journey would be made along narrow waterways under power, and at the sloop's maximum auxiliary speed of five knots it promised to be a very long haul. Recollections stirred uneasily of previous experiences with her on inland waterways, the frantic maneuverings at every bridge, the anguished groundings on every shoal. . . . I thought of all the bridges to be negotiated in six thousand miles, and of all the shoals. . . .

Plainly the sailboat was too deep-drafted, too high-masted and too slow for the intended cruise. A condition that had been obvious from the first, of course, and of which I had been aware, but in a detached manner as if it didn't really concern me; for there is all the difference in the world between knowing something and understanding what it means.

My ideas evolve slowly. And evolution being what it is, there are always a number of dead ends and boss shots on the way. I wanted to make a cruise and had a boat but it took some time for it to dawn on me that the two do not necessarily go together, and what I really needed for the trip was a fast shallow-drafted powerboat.

This meant selling the sailboat and when after a little heart-searching I decided to do so my unusually intelligent decision did not receive the universal acclaim I think it deserved.

"What!" cried my friends, "part with *Felicity Ann* . . . after all you've been through together! You can't do that. . . . She's part of you. Why, she's practically a museum piece."

And if there had been anything calculated to put paid to any wavering doubts, that was it.

As soon as the fitting-out was complete I packed up my belongings and sailed the *Felicity Ann* over to Miami to investigate the small-boat market. I entered the States at West Palm Beach, some seventy miles north of Miami, because the wind dropped to nothing in the middle of the Gulf Stream and the auxiliary engine wouldn't go because — as I discovered later — there was too much water in the fuel. Condensation is always rather a problem in the tropics. If it doesn't take place in the boats' own fuel tanks it will certainly do so in the storage tanks, and although one knows that fuel should be filtered, how many of us ever get round to doing so? The Gulf Stream flows north at an unequivocal clip, sweeping everything with it, and there wasn't much I could do about it but be thankful that enough breeze got up eventually to enable me to sail into West Palm Beach — it might have been Fort Pierce or even Norfolk!

Having a passion for any new experience, I was excited about turning the Grand Tour into a power trip, as this made the venture new in all its aspects for me, new places, new people and a new kind of boat to handle; but at that stage I had not the remotest notion of what kind of a powerboat I wanted, and the dreamboat changed shape several times before it crystallized into an outboard cruiser. My experience at first or second hand of these gay little boats was nil, but I watched them skittering about the Florida Waterways with interest and noted their many obvious and appealing advantages. The initial outlay compared to an inboard cruiser seemed small, the maintenance compared to any other kind of craft seemed almost negligible; and the power unit's being outside the hull would cut down the fire risk and leave a lot more room in the boat. The boats are small enough to go under most bridges, thus eliminating all the agonizing will-he-won't-he opening business, and they draw so little water that even if they do run aground it it not a Coast Guard matter to get them afloat again. And they are fast. Though "fast" at that time, I may say, meant anything over ten miles an hour.

All in all, an outboard cruiser seemed just ideal for my forthcoming cruise, but by the time I knew what kind of a boat I wanted it was too late in the year to think about starting the trip. Setting out from Miami as I planned, the cruise had to begin in late spring or early summer so that by the time I reached northern waters they would be open and free from ice. Then with luck — which one always needs when dealing with weather — I should be able to follow on the heels of summer all the way round to the South again. The protracted fitting-out of the *Felicity Ann* had delayed my arrival in the States until mid-August — which would have been too late to start anyway, and the no less protracted havering over the powerboat question carried me well into fall, so there was nothing for it but to wait for spring.

The sailboat was laid up and I settled down to do my waiting in a character cottage in Fort Lauderdale, about thirty miles north of Miami. The cottage had been evolved from a toolshed-*cum*-garage, bit by bit, apparently by an occupant whose needs overrode his skill and patience. Electrical wiring festooned the walls in dips and loops and it was always an interesting gamble as to whether dinner would cook before the neighborhood fuses blew. Water was introduced into the kitchen by a hose from a lean-to, and the refrigerator shook the whole dwelling with the passion of its pulsations. The hibiscus-covered shower was a short walk across the yard and in full peek-a-boo across the neighbors' fence. In the English countryside or the U.S. backwoods the cottage would have passed without much remark, but in that bang-up-to-date platinum-plush Venice of Florida, Fort

Lauderdale, it was an impudent anachronism and a delight, and living in it had a certain poltergeist fascination in that one was never quite sure what was going to happen next.

Everything went black one morning with a *whoosh* and a *crump* like a small bomb. The cottage wavered and some of the wiring came down. I swallowed my heart and opened the door onto a dense panoply of leaves and branches which covered the house, and crawled out through this instant jungle to be confronted by the woodsman from next door, brandishing his axe and gibbering with embarrassment, for it is tantamount to a bus driver losing his way for a woodsman to miscalculate the fall of his tree.

Nonetheless, despite the distractions, I came down with cabin fever before winter was through, and since the only cure for this is some form of outdoor activity, I took an open fourteen-foot outboard skiff from Fort Lauderdale to Key West, 300 miles round trip, to sample outboard cruising on a minor scale. The weather was atrocious most of the time, windy and cold, and the normally bright rainbow-colored tropical waters looked like a bad reproduction of the North Sea in winter. But I finished the trip absolutely delighted with the whole thing. Outboards were great fun. Like little sports cars, and my idea of fast went up to 15 m.p.h. I looked forward immensely to the Grand Tour and eagerly awaited the arrival of spring, wholly unaware of the events, both good and bad, massing and banking about me, piling up like thunderheads, which were to alter the whole course of my life and delay the journey yet another year.

ii

THE important events of our lives have a way of sneaking up on us without warning. No matter what the lyrics say to the contrary, no bells ring, no lights flash. The guns are silent and the drums don't roll. The day dawns just as any other day and no one says, "Hey, take a good look at this guy — he's going to marry you."

Certainly marriage wasn't on my mind or included in my scheme of things during that period in Fort Lauderdale when I was waiting for spring to come so that I could get on with the journey. I have never been what you might call a homebody. My parents wanted me to be an artist, at least my mother did. She was a singer, and in our house Art was All. I had a small talent for drawing horses, but no one realized, least of all myself, that I only drew them because I loved them so and couldn't have one.

"Not practical in London, dear," my mother used to point out to my utter disbelief. I went to every imaginable length to be with horses and ride them. If someone had offered to remove humanity from the face of the earth and leave me with the horses it would have been O.K.

The situation didn't change much as I grew older. My

resolve to "do something with horses" when I grew up simply hardened, as did my parents' that I should not.

"No daughter of mine," stormed my father, "is going to spend her life as a groom mucking out stables." And if he only knew, no daughter of his had anything like that in mind. My dreams included leading in the winner at Epsom, bred and trained of course by said daughter (though not, unfortunately, ridden to victory by her, seeing the mischance of her sex and the way the growing girl was growing). Alas, these dreams always involved capital, of which there was none, at least not on that scale, and eventually a compromise was reached and I went to the London Veterinary College.

But my heart wasn't in it. Sick and dead horses were no substitute for strong live ones. And then at nineteen, nature took its course. I fell in love with a good-looking student, and to my ineffable surprise, live horses dropped to second place. The boy was in his final year with, as everyone said, a Future before him, but more importantly with a horse at home. I said yes when he asked me to marry him and left dissection with a sigh of relief, only to back out of the wedding.

Marriage when you looked at it closely seemed to have all the earmarks of a trap, and was full of grim-faced people forever talking about "duty" with never so much as a glance at the beautiful shimmering world outside just begging you to go out and put footprints in its snow.

My young man wasn't grim-faced in the least, nor was I, but I suspected most people weren't before they were trapped.

Horses were reinstated, though not with quite the same

careless rapture, and since the blood-and-gut business was definitely out so far as I was concerned, there was nothing for it but to give the artist bit a whirl. I drew horses steadily for about a year; then one day a real artist said with quite extraordinary ferocity, "If I see you so much as starting on one of those bloody animals again I'll tear the whole thing apart, and you too." So it was lucky I discovered flying about this time.

My love for flying was such that all other loves paled beside it as light bulbs in the sun. I lived flying and dreamt it. I haunted airfields, hangars, engine shops, and the science museum, gave up smoking, saved money and eventually, with the generous financial assistance of my long-suffering father, acquired the flying time and necessary knowledge to pass the tests for a commercial flying license. After which I settled down into a hard-working, dedicated, unspectacular pilot, flying, as the phrase goes, "for hire and reward."

When I wasn't flying, I drew planes or wrote about them. I had always written, it was as natural to me as breathing. But several years were to pass before I thought of trying to turn it to account, mainly because I thought fiction was the only "real" writing, and for that I had no bent. I was always far too entranced by the current passion to want to try and "make things up."

And so it might have gone on to the end, but for World War II, a course changer if there ever was one, and the man I married. We were married in 1939, two misfits who had found their forte in the rackety flying of the thirties, both hard to get along with but who got along so well together that marriage was the inevitable conventional outcome.

My husband owned an airport, and was also a pilot, but an amateur one. He was blind in one eye and ineligible for a commercial license. At the beginning of the war, the airport was wanted, but neither of us were. The war effort was very selective then, with no use for women or one-eyed pilots, so we farmed. And our farms grew more and more off-beat until finally we were wresting a subsistence from a Scottish island. In 1949 we left this for the sea, and set out in a seventy-foot ketch, the two of us, to cross the Atlantic. Our ship was lost in the English Channel in a gale, and in the effort to reach land on a raft, my husband perished.

Shock and a number of psychological reasons compelled me to stay with ships and the sea, so that three years later I set out alone in the *Felicity Ann* and sailed to America by way of France, Spain, Gibraltar, Morocco, the Canary Islands and the West Indies, finally arriving in New York in the winter of 1953.

The ensuing five years were spent cruising between New York, Florida and the Bahama Islands and included a brief bout with marriage that didn't take and was, so to speak, struck off the rolls.

By now I realized the world was far too full of exciting things for one to be single-minded (at last I was free to sketch any old thing that took my fancy for the moment). The system of doing what I wanted and writing about it had evolved into a joyous if not particularly prosperous way of life; and all told, I was not discontent with my lot by the time the Fort Lauderdale interlude came up. Certainly nothing was farther from my mind than wedding bells the night I went to dinner at the Steve Trumbulls' in Miami.

Steve and his wife Jane both work on the Miami *Herald.* I had first met Steve when I was maundering along the coast one of those times with the sailboat. He is an astute and sympathetic writer and so cognizant of the state that he has made his home that he is known throughout as Mr. Florida. He is also a keen fisherman, boatman and cook. That night the Trumbulls were giving a chowder party and had gathered round them a company of keen fishermen, boatmen and cooks.

One of them, an ebullient man of medium height and build, of an age I guessed to be near my own, with a bland broad forehead and a droll expression behind his gray-green eyes, said, "I am certainly glad to meet *you*," as if he meant it; but I recognized — or thought I recognized — the normal American manifestation of outgoing quasi-sincerity, which never fails to put the English instantly on guard. In England strangers are guilty until proved innocent, so we are not particularly glad to meet anyone; introductions are made with all parties atavistically weighing the chances of attack. No one is any wiser after an English introduction, because even if they listen they won't know what has been said. We don't like to make ourselves plain in England. Facility of expression to us is irrefutable evidence of charlatanism and is to be avoided at all costs. Americans happily free of this inhibition proclaim the names in an introduction loud and clear, though not to me: I'm still busy weighing up my adversaries. So I had no idea who this was with the gray-green eyes who was so glad to meet *me*.

Our first conversation gave no clue, nor to what Fate had in store either. I had contributed my usual weather banality, some remark about the humidity, and got this in reply: "On the contrary," said he, "it is the humidity that makes it possible to live in Miami. There has never yet been a case of heat prostration here. Sunstroke, yes. But not a single recorded case of anyone dying of heat-stroke. It's the dry heat that's the killer. You sweat and dehydrate without being able to reabsorb any moisture from the atmosphere and suddenly you collapse. Human habitation is only possible in hot moist climates, never in the really hot dry ones."

I was enthralled. I'm not much of a small-talker my-self, and I'd never think of leading to the attack with a one-two like this. Someone mentioned frangipani, and he said, "It comes from south China," and I thought, "My golly, he's off again," but he stopped at that.

Quite against the rules, but because I was so fascinated, I asked him point-blank for his name.

"Bert Billheimer," he said briskly, and next day I was in a frenzy of uncertainty because I had promised to go to a party that night with the Trumbulls and I didn't know if our host's name was Bill Bertheimer or Bert Billheimer.

"Which is it?" I asked as we drove there. Jane put me straight and Steve said, "He's an awfully nice guy. I've known him for years. Ever since we were all in Chicago. He was crazy about sailing Star boats then on Lake Michigan, so I guess that's why they gave him an LCI to play with in the Pacific. He was in the airline business after the war."

"Not any more, though?"

"No, he said it got too dull. In the packaging business now, I believe."

Jane said, "Bert's a doll. Can't imagine what his wife was thinking of. . . ."

"Oh," I said. "Wife?"

"Ex. She decided last year she wanted to be unmarried. No hard feelings, just wanted out. Imagine anyone wanting to be *un*married, especially after nearly twenty years."

I thought to myself that many women after twenty years, having been married young and never having known what it was like to be independent, might feel the urge to stretch their wings, but few have the courage to try.

"Hi, Bill," I said on arrival, stupefied by an absurd shyness.

"Hi, honey-chile," said he, temporarily Southern. "It's Bert, remember?"

"Oh. Eg-, Cuth-, Her- or -ram?"

"What? Oh, -rand, as in Russell. Bertrand."

And that, as they say, is the way great oaks from little acorns grow.

Having met in the company of keen fishermen, boatmen and cooks, it was a *sine qua non* that we should have plenty in common and we were also able to make some exchanges of related interests. Bert introduced me to fly-fishing and I introduced him to skin diving, and we adopted each other's enthusiams with fervor. Bert's love of sailing, which had covered many years of cruising the Great Lakes and the Bahamas as well as racing, had given way of late to power too, although his change was somewhat more sedate than mine. At weekends we would occasionally troll Biscayne Bay for mackerel in the venerable cruiser *Wayward* which he owned in partnership with two others.

We were both mad about cooking, and dinner was the result of combined operations when he used to drive up from Miami after work through thirty miles of rush-hour traffic.

"It must be love," he'd say, ducking through the cottage door to unload a huge paper sack on the kitchen table. Bert always brought a wonderful assortment of comestibles and wines. He said, "Some men give their girls flowers, but I'm the practical type."

After some weeks Bert said, "Are you really going on this old trip?" And I said, "But of course. I must. Everything's organized for it now. I'm taking off at the end of May."

Which shows how little I knew. At the end of May I wobbled out of the hospital, and Bert and I were married the following month.

The hospital stint was entirely unexpected. There had been warnings enough, I suppose, but symptoms are only recognizable in others, never ourselves. *They* are the ones that should see a doctor, not us. (Don't fuss, you know I always get a headache on Thursdays. This is my Thursday headache. It will go away.) Even when the headaches come on Tuesdays as well as Thursdays we merely adjust ourselves and accept it philosophically, and it isn't until the headaches appear every day, all day, and we are practically incapacitated that we think maybe it is time to see a doctor.

The sound of the Miami downtown traffic filtered through the doctor's office, muted and unreal, as he told me the results of the biopsy. It was cancer, he said in a roundabout way. And I would have to have an operation. He explained it all very carefully and drew maps so that I would understand something of what would have to take place. It was impossible to think of it as having any reference to me. All I could think of was, pooh, you're far too young and good-looking to be a doctor, what do you know about it? And out loud I said, "But I can't have an operation. I haven't time. You see, I am going away on a trip at the end of May. In a boat."

Bert drove me to the hospital and missed visiting but one day of the ten weeks I was there, when he went, so apologetically, poor dear, sailing for the weekend. I treasured these visits and marveled at them because I cannot abide sickness myself. I do not know how to comport myself with sick people, how to talk to them. They are no longer the people I know and I earnestly wish they would hurry up and get better and become their proper recognizable selves again. The common defense of sickness—"I cannot help being this way"—has always seemed somewhat suspicious to me. Even more so now that I've been ill myself. Illness creates the perfect state for that wretched little ego. There are no worries for the sick. None of the petty tyrannies and anxieties of everyday life. No responsibilities. Nothing matters. Nothing is more important than the gratification of an immediate physical need; a drink of water, or a state of no-pain. One is justifiably the center of one's own micro-world, one is safe from criticism, and *so cherished.* If in everyday life there was displayed but one-tenth of the dedicated devotion, compassion and loving kindness that doctors and nurses give their patients, the danger of that hideous mushroom cloud making its calamitous appearance might be considerably lessened. And the thought occurs that perhaps everyone ought to have at least one walloping illness in his life to appreciate that there *is* this great feeling inherent in mankind for his fellow men, a feeling that at a pinch will override every other emotion and which might be called love if "love" wasn't the most cruelly misused word in the English language. A sojourn in the hospital is an illuminating experience, albeit a sobering and a humbling one.

Convalescence took about a year. Bert and I made our home in Miami — safe from heat prostration! — where, as he put it, Bert packaged up a storm during the week and I hibernated in a convalescent dream-world. On weekends we browsed about the local waters, furthering an acquaintance with outboard motors on a fourteen-foot skiff that we were reduced to after Bert had separated himself from the cruiser.

Then spring came round again. . . .

"I love your little boot-box home and I don't see how you can bear to leave it," said Mercy, "and your new husband and all. Oh dear, Ann, I thought we'd got you safely settled with Bert and that you'd be through with all this nonsense, rushing about in boats. Bert, can't you stop her?"

"Of course he can't," said Alan with the special twinkle he reserves for what he calls his wife's mother-hen proclivities, "nor can you. Haven't you learned that yet?"

Alan and Mercy Stearns had been my first friends in the States and are two of my dearest, and on this, their first visit to our ménage in Miami, they were surprised and concerned to find preparations going ahead for the Grand Tour.

"Go with her, Bert," urged Mercy.

"I can't take that kind of time off, Mercy," said Bert, adding with a grin, "Besides, she won't let me — her writing contracts say she has to go alone. They don't want a man along — spoil the story."

"Oh, fiddlesticks," said Mercy, "things are different now. She's been ill. What does the doctor think about this?" She turned to me fiercely.

"The doctor thinks it's fine," I said, "I'm not ill any more. And if I don't make the trip, how am I ever going to repay the royalty advances?"

And how can I ever get back on my feet, I thought, for I was at that critical stage of convalescence when physical recovery has outstripped the return of self-confidence. Of all the attributes, self-confidence is the most hardly won and the most easily lost. A long illness insidiously chips it away to a sliver, and there comes a point during recovery when you realize that if you don't make the effort to throw off the lethargy of dependence you'll become a professional invalid and lost forever.

Apart from my commitments concerning it, the Grand Tour still looked good to me, and I felt it might be just the thing to get me out of my mental wheel chair. I would have to rely on my own resources, make my own decisions, meet my own problems and so reinstate myself as a person to myself. Thus the sublime is so often reduced to the ridiculous. That grand scheme I had of going in search of America ended up by my going in search of myself. Though it could be argued, I suppose, that this is the basis for much journeying.

Marriage had inevitably altered my approach to the trip. A measure of detachment might have been possible in my observations had I been able to make the journey when first planned, as a visitor and a single "gal." But the anthropological touch "This is your home and how you live in it" was impossible now that it was my home too. You look at a house when you are going to live in it very differently from the way you do when you are simply visiting there.

"It is not a dangerous trip and I won't be away so long," I protested to Mercy's persistently dubious expression. "Bert and I are going to have a date on the telephone at seven o'clock on every Monday and Thursday night, and whenever he can he's going to drive up some place and meet me."

"Well, you'd better make it at our house for the first time," growled Mercy, "and I don't care what you say, I still think you're nuts."

iii

IN THE outboard field boats and motors do not as a rule come together, at least not when they are new. You buy your hull and motors separately and either put them together yourself or have it done professionally. In the case of a small skiff the assembling is simple, but larger boats with more complicated gear are better put together with the professional touch.

The boat finally chosen for my Grand Tour was a seventeen-foot Glass Magic "Ranger Fiesta," a very pretty little Fiberglas outboard cabin cruiser. She was blue and white, a convertible with a folding canvas top over the cockpit. On the trial run to Key West in the fourteen-footer I had stopped at a motel each night, but on this trip I intended to live aboard. The Glass Magic boat was roomy enough to enable this to be done on a comfortable camping level. By an ingenious arrangement of a folding canvas cot and the readjustment of a table top to fill the floor well in the cabin, it was possible to sleep three in the cabin, though why anyone should want to I cannot imagine. Anyway, I intended to sleep only myself and needed every available inch for gear above the normal domestic and maritime needs, such as drawing, writing and photographic equipment, so I dispensed with the extra people sleepers.

In the cabin was a compact sink and head unit on the starboard side, a water tank under the seat amidships, and a settee with a locker under it on the port side. The cockpit and cabin were unusually well supplied with lockers and there was a mirror on the bulkhead by the door, a vanity touch to warm the heart of a gal.

There was an electric light fitting in the cabin, but in order to save the battery I took along an extension cord for use when an electrical outlet was available, a lantern with a large dry battery and a flashlight which glowed at one end in the dark for easy finding.

Two small single-burner stoves, packed in rubber bags, were put aboard and stowed wherever convenient. Stowage aboard the outboard was a casual affair after the complicated preparations prior to going to sea in a sailboat. In fairness one must admit the conditions are very different, but all the same I was surprised to find out how little disturbed everything was below, on the occasions when it was proportionately rough. Of the stoves, one was electric for use in marinas where it could be hooked up to shore current, and the other was a compact Coleman picnic stove. This works like a miniature gas stove and the heat is provided by a little can of propane gas, obtainable at most hardware stores, that looks like a bug bomb or hair spray. It is most effective. It was originally included as an emergency measure but in point of fact got far more use than the other. It was easy, reliable and clean to operate, and to my mind marks a major advance in the outdoor cooking field.

Accustomed to the dim interiors of sailboat cabins where the admission of daylight is rationed through small portholes, I was somewhat daunted at first by the picture-window effect in the cabin. Not being the goldfish type, I quickly ran up a set of curtains to mask the bowl and hung them, threaded on light line, on plastic hooks glued to the side of the boat. No matter what adhesive was used (and in time I tried most of them), sooner or later the right conditions of heat and moisture combined to soften the cement and one by one the hooks lowered themselves on long threads of glue, giving a most peculiar effect. I came to look upon putting up curtain hooks as part of the normal maintenance routine.

When it came to the question of horsepower for the boat it would have been better if I had never done any sailing at all, for experience tends to constrict the viewpoint where subjects appear to be related. In truth, outboard boats and sailboats have nothing in common but the water they float on. To drive the cruiser I had chosen two Evinrude 18-hp motors. I was familiar with this motor and had found it to be reliable, quiet and economical, my favorite features in an engine. Two motors are a necessity for cruising entirely under power and I thought that thirty-six horses would be plenty muscle for a seventeen-foot boat. Bert was old-fashioned too, and thought along similar lines. Two 18's, we agreed, were not only enough; they were bordering on the extravagant—a view not shared by the Santana Marine Service, the firm that was installing the motors and fitting out the boat.

The Santana Marine Service, situated at Dinner Key on Biscayne Bay just below Miami town, is a classic example of the modern boatyard. It has a sales, repair, storage and launching service, mainly for outboard boats, which have revolutionized boating in the U.S. and changed the atmosphere of boating for the brisker.

A boatyard used to be a kind of club where people hung about gossiping and fiddling with their boats, putting off sailing for as long as possible because it was such a project to go out. Now there's no hanging about, there aren't any docks to hang about on, there's a ramp and a launching slip under the hoist and a queue waiting for both. People keep their boats on trailers either at home or at the yard, and when they want to go boating they simply launch and go. It makes for a healthier occupation but gives the old-timers fits because there is no one now to listen to their gallant tales of yore.

Carlo Roncallo, an impetuous Genoese who presides over the Santana affairs, is an enthusiastic outboard driver who thinks nothing of whipping an outboard across the Gulf Stream singlehanded. He said the 18's were of course fine motors, but too small for the boat, and if he were making the trip he would not think in terms of anything less than two 35's. Bert and I smiled at one another at this. We knew all about this hot-rodding about on the water and it wasn't for us. No sir. We old cruising hands knew a thing or two and one of them was that you couldn't often go batting along at 20 m.p.h. with a boat. The 18's would do just fine. Oh well, there's always a few balloonists about to shake their heads at the Wright boys.

To find out what was needed in the way of detail equipment or minor alterations, the motors were hooked up temporarily, a couple of six-gallon cans slung aboard, and Bert and I drove down to the Upper Florida Keys for a weekend. Right away we learned the vital necessity of screening the cabin.

I had heard of "clouds" of mosquitoes and always thought it was poetic license. But a west wind brought mosquitoes out of the Everglade swamps and they came in clouds all right. Thunderheads. They landed in clouds too, so that one didn't just slap here and there, one scooped them off in black handfuls. And the sound of clouds of mosquitoes hungry for blood is unnerving. We drove round in circles all night in self-defense. And "screens" topped the list in the morning.

But the little boat charmed us. She handled beautifully, and did not skid on the turns or pound or show any inclination to broach or dive, features I came to appreciate more and more as my experience of this type of craft grew. Other findings over the weekend were cruising speed of 16 m.p.h., top speed 22 m.p.h., and an approximate fuel consumption of three gallons an hour for both motors. To our sailboat way of thinking, this was high performance, but Carlo Roncallo continued to shrug when we said so.

Because of the twin motor installation we christened the boat *Gemini* after the constellation Gemini, the "Heavenly Twins," but it seemed to inspire people to ask if my birthday is in June, which would suggest that astrology is more popular than astronomy.

Anticipating the many stretches on the cruise where fuel pumps would be few and far between, two eighteen-gallon tanks were installed under the motor well, and two six-gallon emergency tanks in the cockpit. Two batteries, one as a spare, were installed between the two main fuel tanks, and an electric pump took care of the bilge, which this installation made otherwise inaccessible. The division between cockpit and motor well of the Glass Magic cruiser was sturdy and of a proper height to give protection from following seas.

Cockpit equipment included an impressive array of clocks and switches, tachometers, speedometer, ammeter, fuel gauges and a compass. The steering wheel was inset centrally like those of fast cars; and the manually operated windshield wiper brought an old-fashioned snort from Sailor Bert, but turned out to be not only useful but well-nigh indispensable.

Departure day drew near. In order to postpone the separation for as long as possible I had picked a Thursday for the takeoff so that Bert and I could meet that night at the Stearnses' in Fort Lauderdale, and then again the following night further along the way, probably in the Stuart area so that we could spend the weekend boating together.

A couple of days before I was due to leave I went down to Santana's to show *Gemini* off to Steve. Carlo Roncallo met us with a long face and took me aside with such an air of calamity that I was sure the boat must have blown up or somehow disintegrated.

"You can't go," he said. "I can't let you. The boat isn't safe."

He said he had tried her out that morning and that she was nothing less than dangerous.

"Dangerous," he repeated. "It is impossible for you to

go. I cannot permit a boat to go from here in that state. I will not be responsible. . . . There is the reputation of the firm to consider."

Gemini unsafe? What nonsense was this? For a moment I could not think what he was talking about. I thought he had gone mad, or was kidding, pulling one of those last-minute jokes the way people do, and I smiled weakly waiting for the payoff. Then at last I realized he was serious, that there was something amiss. Now that the boat was loaded with all the long-distance gear, the two 18's were not quite horse enough for the job. The boat could scarcely get up on plane at full throttle and there was no reserve power whatsoever.

Then, what to do?

Replace them with two 35's, said Roncallo impatiently, but with commendable restraint, omitting to add "I told you so."

So it's to be changing motors now, I thought with despair; would this show never get on the road? My mind, still under sail, boggled at the prospect. To switch power plants at the very onset of a sailboat cruise would just about put paid to the whole project.

"Oh, no. Not another delay," I wailed.

No, not another delay, promised Roncallo. The boat, he said, would be ready to leave on Thursday as planned. And when Thursday came, sure enough, it was.

It was a gray day, drizzling slightly. Carlo Roncallo, wearing a triumphant smile and a pair of scarlet swimming shorts, stood by the boat under the hoist, and when he saw me, waved at her with a flourish. "You'll like her much better now," he said.

I looked at the new motors. Strangers. And with no nonsense about them. Very stern and handsome and obviously full of latent power. Oozing horsepower. Secretly, I thought they looked too big, out of proportion to the size of the boat, for balance, like beauty, is a matter of custom and emotion, and my eye was not used to outboard motors of this size. (*Seventy* horses for this little boat.)

Gemini was swung into the water and Roncallo, Bert and I went out in her and bumped about on the bay for me to try my hand and see that everything was shipshape for the voyage ahead. The motors boomed and surged with a power I had never known in a boat before and I felt as if I had got hold of a rocket by mistake that might blast off any moment. I would have liked a little time on my own to get used to the feeling, to work up on an acquaintance slowly with the motors and get the apprehension out of my mind before it came out on my face. But there wasn't a chance. Friends and photographers, Steve in his professional capacity, and, astonishingly, town dignitaries were crowded round the launching slip when we returned for Bert and Roncallo to go ashore, and there was the usual confusion attendant upon leave-taking.

"Drop us a card . . ."

". . . spare plugs in the footlocker . . ."

". . . don't forget to look up . . ."

". . . wave . . ."

". . . here's that address of . . ."

". . . smile . . ."

Everyone talked at once. I didn't know which end was

up, what was aboard, or where it was. I hardly knew where I was going, much less why. My normal departure condition.

Bert winked as I cast off. "Good-bye," he roared with all the others, adding in an undertone, "See you tonight."

It doesn't take long to adapt oneself to anything new if it happens to make life easier. There's almost no problem in making the switch to automatic transmission, washing machines and shallow-draft high-powered boats. By the time I got to Fort Lauderdale I had come to terms with the 35's and they had shrunk to exactly the right size. It was wildly exhilarating to bank on the turns, spring up on plane, to fly along the surface of the water; it was like recapturing some of the old thrill of flying, and I thought, "I'll never want to settle for less again." On the Dania measured mile I let her out and clocked 33 m.p.h. and the top came off the limits to my idea of fast.

The Stearnses' house was on a canal off the New River in Fort Lauderdale and Alan was on the dock to meet me. They had recently moved there, and he said their own dock was not yet ready and directed me to tie up at another, belonging to an amenable but absent neighbor further down the canal where it joins the river.

Bubbling over with greetings and queries, wearing a gay implausible apron, Mercy came on the scene just as I was climbing ashore. Looking at the cabin door left open, she said, "Aren't you going to lock up?"

"Lock up?"

Alan frowned. "I wish our dock was ready," he said; "we could keep an eye on her all the time then. Everyone's away here. But she ought to be safe for one night. . . . Your motors are padlocked, of course?"

"Good heavens, no." I was surprised. This was wartime talk in England — about cars — don't forget to lock it up and take the key — not boat talk at all. But the Stearnses seemed genuinely concerned.

"You must get padlocks before you leave in the morning," said Mercy, and Alan said, "There's been so much trouble lately. A lot of outboard motors have been stolen."

"Here?" I looked around incredulously at the charming residential scene, unobtrusively redolent of the discipline money can buy.

"Young punks," said Alan, "they cruise the canals at night without lights and lift what they can from boats at moorings — fittings, motors, anything. They caught one kid who had been working with an aqualung. He'd a cache of thirteen outboard motors hidden under one of the bridges."

"Well, for heaven's sake." But I was in too good a mood from the drive up in the new boat to feel seriously alarmed, and the surroundings seemed so secure. As a gesture I closed the cabin door and went up to the house with Alan and Mercy to await the arrival of my husband.

The robbers came after dinner. It was about half past nine and quite dark. We were sitting round discussing past and present ploys in a room that opened out on to the garden and looked across the canal. *Gemini*, being farther down the canal, was out of sight and, at that stage of the game, somewhat out of mind. Suddenly, though without attracting attention, Alan got up and went outside. Then he called Bert, quietly, as if he wanted to show him something. Bert went out. Mercy and I went on talking. Then Bert yelled. And there was an answering burst of outboard motors. Mercy and I were outside at the double. And all I could see down the canal was the white glint of a wake rolling round the bend and up the river. I thought, *Gemini*'s gone, but Bert, who had run ahead to her moorings, called, "It's all right — she's still here."

Alan phoned the police as I checked the boat. There was nothing missing, for which thanks was entirely due to Alan. None of the rest of us had paid any attention to the sound of an outboard idling down the canal, but it had sounded furtive to Alan. When it stopped he figured it was time to investigate. "It was alongside your boat then," he said, "and there was someone climbing aboard."

Bert said, "Maybe I should have kept quiet and tried to sneak up on them." We debated whether the marauding boat had one motor or two and decided it sounded like one large one, such as a 50-hp. The police called back in remarkably short time to say they had picked up three youths on the river driving a big outboard with no lights. It was the only boat operating on the river and the timing of their whereabouts was about right, but there was of course no question of identification, and as there was nothing missing from *Gemini* that was the end of it.

"Well, anyway," said Mercy, "we can all get a good night's sleep now. They won't try again tonight."

Progress in a specific field can often be measured by the parallel development of illicit enterprises, and on this basis outboard boating can be said to have arrived, at least in the wealthier communities, for it was only in those areas on my travels that I was to hear complaints of large-scale stealing of motors, boats and fittings. In small fishing ports and communities where boats were an indivisible part of life and valued accordingly, they were still inviolable. The Fort Lauderdale incident was the only one of its kind to touch me personally, but I did not take any chances; *Gemini* carried her share of padlocks.

The following night Bert drove up to meet me at Salerno, another sixty miles north on the way, and an attractive fishing and boating center on an offshoot of the St. Lucie River, near where the St. Lucie and Indian Rivers meet to go out to sea. It is a lovely boating area and we made the most of it over the weekend. We scooted up the Indian River to Fort Pierce to visit friends, marveling at the way *Gemini* ate up the miles, and scooted back again to the inlet where we anchored and swam. Seeing that the Atlantic was right by our elbows, we were mildly surprised to discover the surface water was fresh (until Bert consulted his built-in encyclopedia and came up with the information that salt water is heavier). We drove into Stuart for stores, right into the heart of town by pretty little Frazier's Creek, navigable only for small boats. We drove up the St. Lucie River to Pruitt's Fishing Camp for fly-fishing and were met on the way by a fourteen-foot alligator. It teamed up with us and swam chummily alongside and accepted offerings of bread, masticating slowly with great chompings of its long jaws. I thought the spectacle amusing, but a passing fisherman was horrified. "Don't feed that beast," he cried.

Long before I had reached Salerno I had succumbed without a struggle to the ease and delight of outboard cruising. Bert, at the beginning of the weekend, was still humoring me, but the fun we had with the boat broke down most of his reservations. "Say, you really *go*," he said, taking his turn at the wheel and trying not to look too thrilled. For the first time I could see he envied me the trip.

Then suddenly the weekend was over. It was Sunday night and Bert was on his way home. I put away the swim fins and fly rod and got out the charts for the morrow. The Grand Tour was about to begin.

iv

A LONG cruise is like an orange, easier to handle in small sections, with each section being treated as complete in itself. This ensures a measure of control and simplifies much of the detailed organization — charts, for instance. To have put aboard at Miami all the charts needed for the entire trip would not have left much room for anything else. At the end of each sub-cruise, I planned to ship the used charts home and buy new ones for the next section, and within the normally amorphous limits of such planning this is what I managed to do — quite often.

I wanted to keep the cruise as flexible as possible, to alter course and choose the stopovers as moved by expediency or desire, but the terminal points of each section of the cruise were decided on beforehand and only changed by direct necessity. No one dislikes rigidity of purpose, set plans and routine more than I do. I have an almost pathological aversion to roast beef on Sunday and dinner with Aunt Sue on Friday as an immutable fixture. I want to feel free to skip dinner or skip off to Bora-Bora at a moment's notice. And the important thing is not the skipping but the feeling one can. However, accomplishment imposes some limits and all projects are bound to operate under a minimum plan; otherwise they get out of hand, lose direction, turn into something else or fizzle out altogether. So even if I did not stay at the foreordained terminal point I called there for mail, and this ensured that I worked my way back to Miami and didn't find myself wandering up by Nova Scotia somewhere because it had looked so nice on the St. Lawrence. The idea that I should *catch up* on mail at these mail ports was a big laugh. I've never caught up on mail in my life and judging by the growing mound on my desk right now, dating back at least two years, I never will. But they were good places to reorganize or consolidate, stock up, rest or forget the whole thing.

The cruise fell naturally into nine sections, not equidistant, but each covering an area having conditions peculiar to itself. The first section was Miami to New York, a distance of approximately 1400 miles by the Intracoastal Waterway — farther than it is from Land's End to John o' Groat's, the longest haul overland in Great Britain and consequently a standard there for long distance. No British visitor to the States can ever quite grasp the magnitude of the country. He will travel all the way across from the East coast to the West and still believe it is a trick of some sort — a bending of the light rays perhaps, the Americans are always up to something — because obviously it is impossible to have all that land underfoot in one country.

The Intracoastal Waterway between Miami and New York is a wonderfully varied, interconnected series of rivers, lakes, canals and sounds, magnificently maintained by the U. S. Army Corps of Engineers, and casually taken for granted by the thousands of yachtsmen using them. For most of the way the Waterway runs parallel to the Atlantic Ocean, at times being separated from it by little more than a sand dune. Sometimes the barrier is a group of islands, which may or may not be developed into resorts. Sometimes the Waterway strikes out inland, funneling its way though a narrow canal as it does in the lonely but not so dismal Dismal Swamp in Virginia, or it may turn seaward, or cross a wide sound almost out of sight of land. For seventy or eighty miles at a stretch the Inland Waterway winds through sawgrass swamp or wild forest with nary a glimpse of a beer can, billboard or gas pump. There's nothing but buzzard, deer, 'coon and squirrel to note your passing, where turtles sun themselves on rocks, moccasins slide into the water, and, incongruously, a porpoise sounds beside your boat to show the sea is not very far away. But in South Florida man presents a solid front along most of the Waterway.

The Inland Waterway meanders through small towns, new towns and old towns — St. Augustine, Florida, was a going concern in the sixteenth century — and bustles through a busy metropolis like the Navy town of Norfolk, Virginia, but it doesn't quite make it to New York. It peters out at Manasquan, New Jersey, where you must go out past the sea walls into the Atlantic Ocean to finish the last twenty miles to Sandy Hook, and if you happen to have just traversed the New Jersey Waterways over a weekend you will be only too happy to do so.

In the early days of the cruise after leaving Salerno, I was busy adjusting. Driving hour after hour, day after day, was a brisk business, more demanding and quite different from the previous weekend wandering, for all the scooting we did from point to point, and quite different too from any cruising I had ever done before. I found there were still a few old-fashioned notions to shed. One was what constituted a good day's run. In sailboat days under power on the Intracoastal Waterway it had been fifty miles a day, and that had meant a dawn-to-dusk operation. With *Gemini* I figured it should be possible to make a hundred miles in a day without straining anything; accordingly, on leaving Salerno at six o'clock on Monday morning I set my sights for Titusville. Before noon I was in Titusville, which was ridiculous. Much too soon to call it quits, so I drove on, computing the most fantastic daily averages, and ran out of gas in the Mosquito Lagoon on the far side of the haul-over Canal. I had overlooked, shame on me, the relationship of hours per gallon to rpm. The main tanks had run out after six hours' running. Over the weekend they had given nine hours' running and that was what I was expecting to get from them. I had overlooked that our weekend driving had included a lot of slow running and that slow running makes the gas *last* longer, although mileage is not necessarily increased. In other words, roughly speaking, a given amount of fuel is good for so many miles, irrespective of speed. I switched to the emergency tanks and drove to New Smyrna Beach to refuel. I finally called it a day at the north end of Daytona Beach, after having driven 145 miles. There were still a few hours of daylight left, but it seemed a good idea to use them for shopping and a look round.

I noted that in places, speed improved the scenery.

The dull stretches that had seemed so interminable at 5 m.p.h. were over before there was time to get bored, though speed makes pilotage a lively affair, flinging finger-posts, buoys and landmarks at you in quick succession, demanding instant decisions with barely a moment to consult the chart. But speed can also be hypnotic on still, bright days when the water is like a mirror. The motors drone a lullaby and before you know what's up you're out, asleep. I fetched up on a sandbank in Georgia this way. It was so hot, so smooth, so bright, there was no traffic, nothing to disturb, no sound but the steady soothing song of the motors, and pretty soon there . . . was . . . nothing. . . . Then suddenly the boat stopped short, the motors were up and screaming at the top of their rpm, and I woke with a start. Shocked, dismayed, chagrined, cross, automatically I went into the old routine for getting-boats-off-that-have-run-aground, then remembered the kind of boat I was in and with enormous relief picked up the boathook and pushed off. Once you know about "parkway" hypnosis on the water you can take steps to combat it, create your own distractions, sing (which can be pretty distracting if you are me), take deep breaths, or drop the hook and sleep it off. It is only likely to become seriously troublesome for the single-hander, and there don't seem to be many of those about.

On the negative side, speed seems to have a regrettable effect on human nature. Perhaps it steps up the mental metabolism, but whatever it is, it certainly creates a false feverish impatience from which none of us seem to be immune. Any motorist stalled at a green light is instantly aware of this phenomenon. I was trapped behind a cruiser in a narrow channel for twenty miles and you'd have thought I was madly trying to get that news from Ghent to Aix the way I was carrying on. She was a big cruiser without a sea-kindly line in the whole of her design, and her great square box of a stern left a wake like the surf breaking over a bar in a nor'wester. I couldn't get past her because you had to treat her wake like surf and run it squarely, at right angles, but *that* put you out of the channel into only a few inches of water, too shallow even for the Heavenly Twins. As a rule, in such circumstances, the leading boat will slow down to reduce his wash and let the overtaking craft go ahead. But not this boy. He plowed on relentlessly at 12 knots, a hideous speed for an outboard, causing it to squat and advance in a pregnant manner pushing all before it.

The fact that 12 knots was just twice as fast as I had ever been able to go on the water before (and then only when everything was "downhill") did nothing to alleviate my impatience. I shudder to think of the tempers outer space travelers are going to have.

There were times, however, when I chose to amble along, gazing at the view, at a sober five knots, which *Gemini* did comfortably enough. Lying flat on the water like any old barge, she was a sight to madden small boys on the bank.

"What's the matter? Won't she go any faster?" they would cry, eating with envious eyes the motors, smart and racy-looking in their blue-black and white hoods, and obviously wasted on an old crow like me. "Aw, c'm on," they'd beg, "Show us how fast she'll go." And of course, old Ham Davison would oblige, making rocket takeoffs, banked turns and all that stuff, lapping up, I'm sorry to say, the applause.

As the Grand Tour was not to be a fastest or farthest type tour, but a Grand Sight-Seeing Tour, I saw no point in traveling at night, which is not a very feasible procedure for small fast boats with neither crew nor searchlights. The logs, coconuts, palm fronds, submerged stakes, spoil banks, and bends in the river which present no difficulty in daylight are apt to give trouble in the dark. Besides, one has to sleep and in my opinion the evening has not been improved upon for this. So nightfall found *Gemini* tied up or at anchor someplace, and as the Intracoastal was not entirely unfamiliar I tried to find new places to stay each time. One of these was Jekyll Island, on the South Georgia coast, connected to the mainland by a bridge and right on the Waterway. The citizens are welcoming people, very anxious to promote their lovely island and very proud of its democratic progress.

As one of the Park Rangers put it, "There used to be nothing here but little old millionaires' houses." Now it is a state park, a resort for everyone, and the little old millionaires' houses are museums and hotels.

I had read somewhere that there was good shelling to be had on the beach and this was an enticement I could not resist.

A toy train trundles along the road between the marina and hotel on the Waterway across to the beach on the ocean side, to carry weary holiday makers to and fro. Actually, it is not far to walk across the island at this point and it is very pleasant to wander along the grass verges that lie between the road and the woods that stand so thickly on either side.

A deer, poised in a clearing, peered at me as I walked past. He seemed interested and unafraid.

The shelling was disappointing, but that isn't to say it was overrated. A beach haul of shells is variable and depends on many factors, time of year, tides, and recent weather, and a beach that offers collector's pieces on one visit may not produce half a shell another time. But the hunt is worth almost as much as the treasure, and the beach at Jekyll Island is truly magnificent. Miles and miles of hard white sand, similar to the famous beach at Daytona, and the kind of wonderful natural resource that man can't keep his hands off. Already there are a boardwalk, a restaurant, and a fairground with swings, merry-go-rounds and switchbacks. Motels and shopping centers cannot be far behind. There are lifeguards, garbage cans, barbecues, picnic tables and seats. And, fountainhead of U.S. civilization, fresh running water. Standpipes situated at intervals of a few yards all along the front. Everything, in fact, for you to spend a day by the sea almost as you would at home.

V

I WAS still in what is known as the Deep South — a strange expression, as if by inference the North was shallow — when one of the motors manifested a slight indisposition, and being of the forewarned-forearmed school when it comes to anything mechanical, I stopped at an outboard service station, fortuitously on hand by late afternoon, to have it checked.

Waterside "garages," catering to the small-boatman, offering quick service and ready-mixed fuel for outboard motors from conveniently low floating docks, had mushroomed along the Waterway since last I had passed that way. A sign of the times and a vast improvement on the old-style, long-legged, shell-encrusted jetties, but I wondered if they were all manned by long lean laconic young men because the business attracts that type or do the men get that way by association? In all my travels I have never met a fat loquacious outboard motor mechanic, and if I ever do I'll probably suspect his efficiency.

The owner of this operation was unexpectedly, but quite unmistakably, a New Yorker.

He was tall and handsome, smooth and suave, and

wore his overalls with a distinctly metropolitan air. He welcomed me courteously and was quite fascinated when I explained what I was doing.

"All by yourself," he exclaimed. "Wonderful! Does Ralph know you are doing this?"

Ralph? I looked blank.

"Ralph Evinrude."

Oh, ah. The "father" of my motors. "No, I don't believe so. Should he?"

"Of course. I'll tell him. He's coming here tonight—well, not exactly here, he's staying further down the river where there's more water for his yacht. I'm having dinner with him. On board the *Chanticleer*. You've been aboard her of course? No? Oh you should. What an experience! What a ship! What a lovely ship. She has everything, but everything. Frances is with him. You've met her of course? Frances Langford, his wife? A lovely girl. A really lovely girl."

He looked down at the boat. "All the way from Miami," he said, shaking his head as if I had already traveled thousands of miles instead of only a few hundred. "Miami . . . let me see, maybe you know my old friend there, Ron . . . Ron . . ." he snapped his fingers, "Roncarlos."

"Carlo Roncallo."

"Yes. Carlos. A great boy. I haven't seen him since . . . I'm going to call Ralph right now and tell him about you. Perhaps he'll ask you to dinner."

Perhaps not, I thought hopefully, for I was finding a little to my dismay that I had still a lot of leeway to make up in physical strength. Eight or nine hours driving and that was it. No swinging on the chandeliers after dark for me. A short walk and a brief exchange with the locals and I was ready to put out my social lights and go to sleep.

"Ralph says he would be delighted if you would join us for dinner this evening." The voice was formal as befitted the message. I wriggled off the bunk and poked my head out of the cabin. "Why, that's fine," I said. The father of my motors. A royal command. "I'd love to. Will you pick me up here?" I imagined we'd be driving to wherever the yacht was docked and thought, well anyway, I'll get a rest riding in the car. But that was not to be. . . .

"We thought if you wouldn't mind, we could all go down in your boat. I know Ralph would love to see it."

"Of course," I said. "Splendid. The only trouble is that I don't drive at night if I can help it. I've terrible night sight. Blind as a bat . . ."

"That's O.K. I'll drive."

I hate being driven, but grinned with fury and said "Great," and a time of departure was agreed. It just about gave me time to tidy up and change, a process that aboard a small boat requires enormous effort and takes about three times as long as usual. It wouldn't be so bad if it wasn't for this ridiculous modern obsession with personal appearance, and I wished a pox upon the advertising fraternity who have made life so difficult for women today by creating an illusion that women are never tired, bedraggled or cross. Women are always glamorous, gorgeous, good-humored, sexy and twenty years old. There they are, these lovely creatures, everywhere you look, in every magazine and newspaper, on every billboard, television and movie screen, gaily going about their business of the day (some of it highly unlikely too) dressed in the height of fashion, fresh from the beauty parlor, swooning with desire and ineluctably seductive. Which is fine for adolescent males, no doubt, but hard on us poor mortals, who, with every strike against us, inevitably fighting the law of diminishing returns, are expected to go and look likewise. If we don't make the attempt to conform to this drummed-up concept of an Eternal Dream of Fair Women, we are suspect and shunned, for we are probably subversive and undoubtedly *disturbed*. The monstrous campaign has us so in thrall that it does not matter how tired we are, how swollen our feet, how aching our back, how unspeakably fed-up we are with the whole goshdarned works, we hitch up our bras, reef in our girdles, pin up our hair, slap on the warpaint and make with the glamour.

At all costs convention must be preserved. Lipstick on askew is better than no lipstick at all.

Mr. and Mrs. Dealer arrived just as I was pinning up my long and always recalcitrant hair. I had showered and changed and was not much more disheveled than I had been before. The Dealers were very elegant and shipshape in the Manhattan manner, yachting style. Mr. Dealer's white shirt was very crisp and restrained against his dark jacket, and attractive Mrs. Dealer in neat white shorts wore a pert little pudding-basin hat with bees on it that I admired enormously.

"Well," said Mr. Dealer briskly, "shall we go?"

The throttles opened wide with a snap, and *Gemini*, surprised, sprang forward, Yessir, and up on plane. When I was flying for a living I used to do things very slowly. The engines didn't like it if you were rough and it was considered wise to humor them. I can't get out of the way of it, though they say it doesn't matter now.

Flat out, we roared downriver. Mr. Dealer looked at his watch. "Time her over the mile," he said. Then later, "Your speedometer seems to be about right. That's odd." It was clocking 30 m.p.h. Three up and all that load. Good little *Gemini*. We made a swish-tail landing, coming close up by the *Chanticleer* and rolling the wash right up under her stern. Very flashy. Lithe, soft-footed crew members of the huge yacht leapt about cat-like to secure our lines.

Ralph Evinrude, open-faced, beaming and massively Nordic, son of the ingenious Scandinavian responsible for originating the motor that bears his name, greeted us on the gangway.

". . . my wife, Frances. . . ."

Mr. Dealer had not exaggerated. Mrs. Evinrude, blonde, petite, charming, was as delightful off the screen as on, and a pretty aggravating reminder that there may be something in this poster business after all. When I was a small girl and my ego suffered the grievous blows that are wont to afflict the young, I used to comfort myself by saying, "Ah, but you should see me on a horse." Now that I am a big gal and pretty nearly as vulnerable, it would be so nice to be able to solace myself by saying, "Ah, but you should see me on a boat." But alas, how can I with this sort of competition about?

Nor had Mr. Dealer exaggerated about the yacht. The *Chanticleer* was the yacht with everything. One hundred and ten feet of good shipboard living. I doubt if many people do so well ashore. The minute I got aboard I felt a momentary pang—what a pity it is that I am not rich, I would enjoy it so. There is the voluptuous feeling of heavy pile underfoot, the seductive invitation of deep cushions, and goblets at every turn. There were television sets at every turn too, it seemed to me, above decks or below decks; everywhere you cast your eyes it seemed they were cast right back by a TV screen. I guessed that this was probably on account of the professional interest on board, and that Mrs. Evinrude in her capacity as Miss Langford read television screens the way I do books.

Mr. Dealer said, "I hear you've put in stereo since I was last aboard," and our host, with infectious enthusiasm, trotted out his latest hobby-horse. After he had twiddled a few knobs in what I can only think of as an electronic cockpit, we explored the ship to the accompaniment of what seemed like the sound effects from the jungle sequences of *The Bridge on the River Kwai*. (Similar sounds follow you in the South American section of the Natural History Museum in New York. They are weird and quite haunting. And on the *Chanticleer* they seemed to be more disembodied than any sound in real life, coming elusively, like a sonic will-o'-the-wisp, from all around, from overhead, down by your feet, and suddenly from just behind your left ear.)

We wandered along corridors and up and down companionways, through dining rooms and the equivalent of living rooms, dens and patios, through staterooms with full-length mirrors and adjoining bathrooms. We wandered through tremendous kitchens of stainless steel and spacious crew's quarters, through the navigational department where there was every possible device to take the guess out of going, through the engine rooms splendid in white wall-to-wall machinery, and at last on to the boat deck where there were two boats as big as *Gemini* and an impartial array of Outboard Marine's outboard motors. "No favorites," beamed Ralph Evinrude, and pointing with triumph, "How do you like that?" "That" was an absurd but quite irresistible bull-nosed little motor car with basket seats and a top with a surrey-type fringe. It stood chocked, so that it couldn't roll, by davits, ready to be swung ashore.

"Well, *I* like that," said Mr. Dealer, "but the taxi drivers won't."

It was fairly festive on board, with too many people for my British inhibitions to grasp at one fell introduction, and the only ones I could be sure of, outside the Dealers and the Evinrudes, were Ralph Evinrude's son and Mrs. Evinrude's mother. Trust me to keep positive recognition strictly to the family. There was a showing of brass from various boatyards round and about, a number of agreeable young men who may or may not have been part of the crew, and, as the passing of such a vessel could not go without remark, there were newsmen from local papers and radio and television stations, some armed with that formidable modern blackmailer, the tape recorder.

To Europeans conditioned to the Hollywood version, American reporters come as a pleasant surprise. Unlike their screen counterparts they are usually very civil and disarming, and the only thing I have against them is that they are far too clever at drawing one out, with the result that one talks far too much. Who doesn't love to talk—especially about themselves—but who ever wants to listen? So when a legal, moral, non-fattening opportunity to do so comes our way it is well-nigh irresistible. But the talker's remorse afterwards! Fortunately, the American reporter is pretty deft at sifting a few grains of sense from the welter of nonsensical chaff, and makes a story from it that one can read without blanching. Unfortunately, there's not much sifting done with a tape recorder, which is why so many radio and television interviews are quite unspeakably dreary, and it is a never-ending source of astonishment to me the way a radio or television reporter will play back a tape nodding his head and looking as rapt as if he were hearing angel voices.

At least what one writes is considered nonsense, but what one says on the spur of the moment makes one wonder whether we are really ready for speech yet.

The pleasant evening passed quickly and it was late

when we got up to go. It was a very dark night and Mr. Dealer stumbled coming aboard *Gemini*. "Can you see?" I asked anxiously, because of course I couldn't. He laughed shortly and said not to worry, he knew the river like the palm of his hand. We took off at full throttle and roared away with the well-wishes from the *Chanticleer* ringing in our ears.

I must say it was very exciting tearing up the river at thirty miles an hour in the dark, but I had to keep telling myself that most people have much better night sight than I have.

About halfway home, by time standards only, the boat went *zonkety-splat-splat-splat* on to a mudbank.

"Tsk," said Mr. Dealer, or words to that effect. "Where did that one come from?" He put the motors into reverse and they swore most dreadfully but failed to move the boat.

The bank was of soft ooze in which even a flat-bottomed boat sinks and holds fast, and from which there is no way of pushing off. For a while the situation looked quite tiresome.

Happily a fishing boat passed by, threw us a line and pulled us off, though not very easily.

And away we went again. Full throttle. I was very tired and more than anything in the world wanted to get home, tie up and sleep, and suggested that maybe we'd get home quicker if we went more slowly. But Mr. Dealer didn't hear so well with the motors going full bore and there was no doubt that he was in a hurry to get home too.

Suddenly the weird wild subway-like drive came to

an end, without mishap moreover, and there we were tied up alongside the dock.

The Dealers went ashore, and we bade each other good night and good-bye, for I was to be away in the morning before they would be about. As they were walking away, Mrs. Dealer turned and whipped off her cute little pudding-basin hat and plonked it on my head. "Souvenir," she said.

I wore it almost constantly afterwards, but I'm afraid it didn't suit me nearly so well.

The *Chanticleer* was making almost the same cruise as the *Gemini*, north to the Great Lakes and back to Florida by the Mississippi and the Gulf of Mexico, but where *Gemini* crossed the "top" of the quadrilateral tour by Lake Ontario and the Trent Canal, *Chanticleer* crossed it via Lake Erie and Lake Huron. But for a while when we were both still in the Southern states our tracks crossed several times. The encounters were not only enjoyable for me but informative; Ralph Evinrude, not unnaturally, was a mine of information about the motors, and since he had been over the course a number of times before, he also imparted a number of valuable tips on the cruise.

When the Fourth of July rolled up I was invited to join the celebration aboard and rendezvoused with the yacht at a broad reach in the river at the north end of Butler Island, north of Georgetown. It's a peaceful spot of innumerable creeks where tall trees fortress the banks of the wide river. Traditionally, a barbecue was held on the afterdeck, over which Frances Evinrude presided with glamorous efficiency. Later in the evening, equally traditional, fireworks were set off. And then I spent the night aboard: "No sense in your going back to your little boat now, you might as well sleep in comfort when you can." It was 6:30 when I awoke in the morning and the *Chanticleer* was under way with *Gemini* lashed alongside, motors up, bumming a free ride. How do I get away? I wondered, for the river was too narrow now for the *Chanticleer* to stop and anchor. Will they drop me like they do those airplane jobs from bombers? Which was precisely how it was proposed I should depart. On the wing. I can't say I was exactly mad with joy at the idea, but as everyone seemed to take it as a matter of course, I pretended to also, and as a matter of fact, it wasn't at all difficult. Having been asked to make a circuit of the yacht for pictures before speeding away, I did so, *ventre à terre*, like a puppy round a Great Dane. My progress was followed by everyone on the yacht, Argus-eyed with cameras. Then I galloped away, breathing easily at last.

As the Southern states rolled away behind us, the Evinrudes and I met less often. Always one or the other of us was ahead, and after Morehead City, North Carolina, I did not see the yacht again. But I would hear of her from time to time, over someone's ship-to-shore. Or sometimes at a marina I'd hear a dockmaster excitedly giving orders: "The *Chanticleer*'s coming in tomorrow — keep the long dock clear." Once at one of the locks on the Erie Canal where lock watching is a popular sport, a bystander said wistfully to me, "A beautiful yacht came through here last week. You should'a seen her. Boy! Belongs to a film star. I saw her. Boy! Was she something! Had her boy friend with her. . . ."

That was his idea of romance and he didn't consider the facts an improvement.

VI

NORFOLK, Virginia, although over 900 miles from Miami, is a psychological halfway point for the small-boatman on the way to New York. From there the going becomes comparatively more difficult. There is a choice of routes. One may go all the way by sea, which is the way I went with the sailboat, or go as far as Cape May by sea and pick up the New Jersey Waterways there. Or one can take the scenic route up Chesapeake Bay to Chesapeake City and cross the neck of the two states, Maryland and Delaware, by the Chesapeake-Delaware Canal, thence to Cape May and the Waterways by the Delaware River. I chose the Chesapeake route as it seemed to offer more interest and protection for a small boat, and was disappointed because I couldn't see the scenery and didn't get a whole lot of protection.

I had heard so much about the Chesapeake Bay area, how beautiful it was, and what magnificent cruising there was to be had there, and the charts looked so inviting, decorated by countless ragged-edged rivers, creeks and inlets, offering endless possibilities for exploration. I had seen a few of the romantic old bugeyes converted to yachts and had conjured up mental pictures of cozy little fishing villages to serve as backgrounds for them, but with one exception, the only things that came up to expectations in the Chesapeake were the fish traps and the squalls.

To appreciate the Chesapeake, it is obvious one must wander there and not simply pass through. The north-south course takes one too far offshore to see much of the landscape, which is more often than not shrouded in fog, mist or haze. This haze was something I had forgotten about in the last few years living in the subtropics, and I longed to be able to give the horizon a good wash and polish so that it would stand out, crystalline and clear, as I had grown used to seeing my horizons. To add to the normally poor visibility of northern latitudes, the weather in the Chesapeake was bad. Not very bad, or dangerous, just plain old lousy—conditions which seemed to have been dogging me since a halfhearted hurricane dragged itself up from the Caribbean to fizzle out in the Charleston area. I had been incarcerated in Norfolk for several days on account of weather, being very depressed by countless old wives' tales about the frightful conditions that can obtain in Chesapeake Bay without a moment's notice. It seemed that if you weren't capsized by a boat-wrecker squall you'd come to grief in the fish traps. Jolly, jolly. These accounts I took with the usual grain of salt because of the inexplicable but unfailing human delight in making much of warnings (the bogey man will get you if you don't watch out), but it made depressing hearing all the same. There was a small-craft warning every morning except one. On this occasion I set out only to see the warning go up as I passed the building where it flies. It took me three hours to cross Hampton Roads — twelve miles. By this time I was fed up with the whole thing and put in to Hampton. A happy move; for it is a charming place, Old World without being quaint, because it is still a working model.

Actually it was bad weather that led me to the one place I found on the Chesapeake that came up to expectations, a place which leads me to believe that the Bay probably has all those charms I have heard about.

"You want good weather to cross the York River in a small boat," they told me at Hampton, and you can see on the chart that it would be a messy place to be caught out, what with the Atlantic behind you, the Chesapeake before you and the York River entrance and Mobjack Bay to the side of you. So I waited a day in Hampton to let the squalls settle, and set out on a morning that didn't exactly fill me with the joy of spring but didn't scare the daylights out of me either. The only trouble I had getting across the York River was in threading my way through the fish traps. On the chart this looks simple: the markers of the fish trap boundaries are clearly sited and plainly numbered. But in real life they are missing in vital spots; the numbers have worn off, the markers have been knocked over and misplaced and are difficult to see in the haze anyway because their black and white colors make an effective camouflage. It isn't impossible, but it takes time for a stranger to sort them out.

At this stage of the cruise I usually stopped at midday to top up the fuel tanks and have lunch. It was a good practice, as it gave me a break and kept the tanks full to meet any adversities in the way of tides, currents or head winds. On the Chesapeake there are not many places one can stop for gas without making a detour of several miles, so naturally I tried to pick gas stops with as little deviation as possible. The first noon stop after leaving Hampton was at Deltaville, but even that required a detour of nearly six miles in and out again. By the time I was out again in the bay, one of those sudden squalls I had been warned about had come up, and it was quite rough. Not, however, too rough to continue, though I noticed a few small boats scurrying for shelter.

I was bound for Fleeton, which had been recommended as a good stopover, but as the afternoon wore on the weather worsened. As I drew near Fleeton it was clear that my arrival there was going to coincide with a father and a mother of a thunderstorm—one of those great gusty blackout affairs with fancy lightning effects; and I could also see that if I continued on the way I would miss the worst of the storm. So I looked at the chart to see what the alternatives were. The most promising appeared to be at Smith Point, right at the entrance to the mighty Potomac River and right in my path. It was not clear from the chart whether I would find any facilities there, but behind the tiny inlet there was plenty of sheltered water in which surely one could find an adequate anchorage. There was enough fuel and stores aboard to see me across the Potomac and to a refueling point in Maryland next day, so I kept on for Smith Point, running parallel to the thunderstorm. It blotted out Fleeton as I passed but spilt only a few drops of rain out my way.

The seas were really churning up by the long sea walls that enclose the narrow entrance to Smith Point. They looked worse than they actually were, though a very strong current swept in between the sea walls. Inside, it was utterly delightful. The inlet widens out and branches off in many directions into charming little creeks and bays where dense pine woods crowd down to the water's edge. There are reeds and sedge and coot and quiet waters; a collection of small fishing boats linked together at moorings; fish nets drying; a few directional stakes unintelligible to the uninitiated.

Sheer curiosity compelled me to follow a series of private markers leading to the Smith Creek Marina and I was glad I did, for this was certainly one of the most delightful spots on this section of the cruise. The marina lies in a lovely peaceful backwater, surrounded by pines. It is a natural, relaxed sort of place with none of the cute pseudo-nautical salty-hearty atmosphere that marks the worst of the yacht clubs and marinas. Refueling, water and ice requirements are taken care of quickly and efficiently and "Anything you want," they offer, "just let us know. There's a guest house and shower on the hill you are welcome to use"; and at that, the social latch is left for you to lift when and if you feel inclined. I found this such a relief, for it is strange how few boating people recognize that the latest arrival in the yacht basin is not necessarily in a brilliantly conversational mood. Personally, I always find it necessary to unwind for quite a while after a day's cruising, and have found the best way of doing so is to get on with the evening chores immediately after tying up. Refueling; figuring out the day's run, engine hours and fuel consumption; studying charts for the next run; and cleaning up the boat gradually restore one to the normal human level of communication. Visiting a boatman the minute he's docked and expecting him to respond to the "who-dat" cross-fire questioning with éclat is like visiting a housewife at the end of the day when she's feeding the twins, bathing the baby and fixing the old man's dinner, and expecting her to scintillate socially. Any mariner designated a "bad-tempered son-of-a-bitch" I suspect may only have been called on too soon.

Smith Point Marina, being the sort of place it is, attracts people who like the kind of thing it offers. It was a happy stop. I loved the place and was loath to leave it.

As far as possible, I tried to make my stops away from big towns and off the beaten track, partly from personal preference, and partly because it is impossible to find fresh material in a one-night stand at places so well known or hackneyed that one is unavoidably prejudiced by prefabricated opinions. So rather than stay in the vicinity of Annapolis, I chose what appeared to be a quiet little harbor south of it, a country place, nowhere near a town. Another Smith Point, I hoped.

It turned out to be the biggest boat basin I'd ever set eyes on, and it was crawling with boats. I drove round the basin for fifteen minutes just staring. But apparently it was not big enough, for I learned later that it was being enlarged to accommodate another 400 boats. A curious situation was in existence at the gas dock, where the deck from two spans in the middle of the shank of the T was missing. Boats were in all the slips on either side of the shank, and business was being conducted as usual (though under the circumstances rather unusual) at the gas dock on the end of the T. In order, presumably, to prevent people from walking along the dock, high barriers had been erected on either side of the gap, and then in order to enable them to pass, two thin planks had been laid end-to-end to bridge the gap. The negotiation of the planks across the twenty-foot gap, with quite a sizable drop into water, would have been taxing enough for many people, and the inclusion of the barriers made it a highly skilled operation. But all evening a steady stream of boatmen, wives, children and girl friends, able, aged and infirm, laden with ice, hampers and gear, passed to and fro along the dock and went through this circus act. No one fell in, no one even slipped, and no one seemed to mind. They just concentrated and it was absolutely fascinating to watch.

I made my way the rest of the way up the Chesapeake from the big boat basin to Chesapeake City by fits and starts because it was miserably rough and uncomfortable. I kept saying to myself, "If it isn't any better by the time I get to Galesville — or Annapolis — or Baltimore, I'll give up and go in." But by the time I had got there it didn't seem so bad and I'd decide to go on a bit further. In that manner I achieved my objective. Chesapeake City, sounding so imposing, has an unexpectedly backwater atmosphere, though it could hardly be more in the main stream. It lies at the western end of the twelve-mile canal linking the big ports of the Chesapeake Bay area with the big ports of the Delaware River, and huge oceangoing vessels are passing through all day and night long, dwarfing the great bridges so that you think they'll never make it. The big ships steal by so silently on their giant cat feet that the only way one is aware of their passing at night is by the tension on the lines as one's boat is inexorably drawn out by the suction of the undertow.

The consensus appeared to be that the Delaware River is a natural stinker, and the only way to tackle it is to bolt down the big ship channel along with the freighters and get it over as quickly as possible. There was nothing to be gained, I was assured, by playing it cagy and trying to do any wind-dodging in the lee of one shore or the other. There wasn't much in the way of a lee or shelter offered on either side, so just pick your weather and get going down that channel, they said.

It wasn't a scenic trip, and I wasn't looking forward very much to this sixty-mile run to Cape May, so I did not stand upon the order of my going. Instead, I wound up the Twins at 6 o'clock in the morning and trotted down the canal to see what was afoot outside in the river. It was a gloomy overcast morning and the waves in the river were falling all over themselves without any apparent reason. Then I discovered the southwest wind was somewhat more ebullient than I had first thought, and it was quarreling with an outgoing tide. The Delaware is pretty shoal and that always creates a lot of crosscurrents. And of course the channel, constantly whipped up by giant eggbeaters as the big ships plow up and down full steam ahead, never gets a chance to settle. The river is wide and gets wider, and the land is low-lying and soon out of sight, but the channel is easy to follow. One is never out of sight of a buoy or a light, and ticking them off on the chart as you pass gives an encouraging sense of getting somewhere on an otherwise deadly monotonous run.

Gemini, the minnow amongst the big ship whales, did rather well, I thought, to average 10 m.p.h. over the run, particularly as she did so without jolting, pounding or fumbling in the way so many speedboats do in uncooperative waters. She had a comfortable speed for most conditions, and it was generally faster than I would have expected. Actually the boat was safe at a much higher speed in that rough water, but she was not so comfortable, and comfort for me was the operative term.

I entered the Cape May Canal at the Atlantic toe of New Jersey with what turned out to be premature jubilation. "Now I'll be able to make some time," I thought, and looked forward to picking myself a nice quiet place by the sea where I could spend a few hours before nightfall to do some shelling and swimming and some lazy beachcombing. Sometimes I wonder where I get my ideas.

It was a weekend, which probably made matters worse, but if the situation prevailing on the New Jersey Waterways is the shape of things to come in boating, I want *out*, quick. Sink the boat, gimme a desert.

The main trouble is that there are too many boats for the water. Heaven knows how many square miles of water are in those Jersey flats all along the coastline, but it is only a few inches deep, too shallow even for outboards, and the dredged channel is very narrow and winding. The New Jersey fishermen are numerous, enthusiastic and not to be denied. They anchor in the channel or tie up to the buoys and markers and clutter up the fairway so that it is difficult for a stranger to see where he is going or, what is more important, where he ought to go. The traffic is as thick as Broadway or Piccadilly in rush hour, but much more disorderly. The boats travel at top speed all the time — it is astonishing how they do it — and make wild, impulsive, unpredictable and unsignaled alterations of course without any regard or reference to "rules of the road." Water skiers hurtle in and out of other fast-moving traffic and anchored fishing boats, casually shedding skiers as they go. To add to the confusion, small sailboat races are conducted — in the channel — and it is every man for himself with his own right of way.

At the various ocean inlets the number of boats has to be seen to be believed, stem to stern, and gunwale to gunwale. Some of the inlets are really dangerous, but truly, anything goes. In amongst the party boats, charter boats, yachts and cruisers, there are skiffs and you-name-its, overloaded, too small, manned by obviously inexperienced crews, romping out to sea and trouble. They say the accident rate in boating hereabouts is higher than it is on the roads. The miracle to me is that anyone survives.

As demand far exceeds supply on these Waterways

the transient boatman gets little in the way of service or civility, and it is extraordinarily difficult to find an overnight berth for any size boat.

"May I tie up here for the night?"

"Nope."

"Do you know where I can?"

"Nope."

One can buy gas all right, with a queue of gas-hungry boatmen milling about audibly willing you to hurry up and get the hell out, and in at least one place I know of they'll turn real ugly at the sight of a credit card.

However, few things are bad all the way through, and there were a couple of bright spots. I found some of the waterfront architecture quite charming, particularly at Atlantic City, of all places, where colorful Swiss chalet-*cum*-dollhouse structures are built directly on the water and are attractively piquant, posed against the background provided by the skyscrapers of the resort proper on the beach. And at Devers Boat Basin, Sea Island City, in a creek made picturesque by beat-up, net-draped commercial fishing docks where a notice says: "Trespassing at your ownrisk," I was lucky enough to find what must surely be the last stronghold of old-fashioned boating manners.

Ruffled and baffled by curt treatment and impossible pilotage, unable to find anywhere to tie up or anchor (unless I emulated the fishermen and anchored in the channel) I went into Devers expecting to hear the usual "nope" and quite prepared to fight tooth and nail for a night's rest, only to receive the most cordial welcome.

The manager of the basin drove me into town for stores and was so pleasant that at first I thought I must be hearing things.

But Devers was an exception, and nothing short of a hurricane would have prevented me from going to sea at Manasquan, the end of the New Jersey Waterways going north, and the absolute, ultimate, final end of the New Jersey Waterways for me.

VII

GEMINI spun easily over the lazy Atlantic rollers to Sandy Hook. The sea was very peaceful and there wasn't a boat in sight. Fog darkened the Lower Bay of the great harbor of New York, but lifted at the Narrows for a slow unveiling of the famous skyline. The Upper Bay was busy, but it was an orderly bustle, and it was, as always, intensely interesting with a diversity of vessels, large and small. Ferries and excursion boats, tugboats disguised as fenders and barges with shrubs and vines growing on their deckhouses, rusty freighters and lofty liners went about their business, and now new on the scene to me, skittering about amongst the big ships, were myriads of little outboards — water beetles on a giant pond.

Dodging the amazing debris going out with the tide on the Hudson River, I sidled through the narrow entrance into the 79th Street Yacht Basin, the only place on Manhattan a passing boatman can tie up that is "close in." But he can do so only if he has influence, and for once in my life I had.

A press party was being held there for the Crawfords, Tod and his wife and daughter, who were making a family-style cruise of eight thousand miles in a sixteen-foot Larson with a 70-hp Mercury outboard engine. Theirs was a well planned, well organized, well executed tour, a brisk no-nonsense kind of operation at which Americans are so good.

This seemed to be outboard cruise year. Another outfit had passed through not too long before. John Hogg and a companion in a small cruiser powered by another pair of Heavenly Twins (two 35-hp Evinrudes), making a repeat run of a long coast-to-coast trip Mr. Hogg had made some thirty years before. He must have seen some changes made!

The classic remark to make about New York City is that it is a fine place to visit but one wouldn't want to live there, in spite of which some ten million people do. For ten days I joined them and teemed right along, writing and reorganizing for the next step of the voyage and generally dashing about because it is impossible not to without being trapped in a revolving door or causing a jam from one end of the town to the other.

Finally everything was done that should have been done and I was ready to go. But it was with mixed feelings I set out. About a fifth of the journey had been accomplished, and although I was not doing as badly as I had secretly feared, it was not as well as I had secretly hoped. I still got very tired and knew I was missing much on account of devoting my attention to keeping going. I missed Bert sorely and was depressed at the fact that the next part of the trip would put still more distance between us. From now on the country was new to me, and I would be traveling along fresh-water rivers, canals and lakes for several thousand miles until I came out into the Gulf of Mexico at New Orleans. Ordinarily this would have thrilled me to the quick, but now I wondered if I had tackled more than I could physically accomplish. The recent experience of the New Jersey Waterways, which had also been new territory, smoldered. What if they were a foretaste of things to come? I didn't really believe that, but all the same it was with some reluctance that I turned my back on the sea and started up the Hudson River.

PART TWO

Canals

⚓

⚓

i

I NOTICED the small boat romping along beside me a short time after leaving the Poughkeepsie Yacht Club, where I had stopped for gas. I had thought of staying there for the night, but a member of the club advised against doing so because there was no protection from the lively wash of commercial traffic. He suggested I would do better to go on up river for another ten miles to Norrie's Yacht Basin at Indian Kill, but advised me to telephone first as "they tend to get jammed up in the evening." (Oh dear, I thought, this again?) "If they can't fix you up," said the member, "I'll arrange for you to have a mooring here, but it will be a restless night if you plan to stay aboard." However, Norrie's had space available if I was going to be there by six o'clock, so I set out to capture it before anyone else. It was drizzling. The boat that caught up and rode beside me was completely hooded by a canvas top and side curtains, and I could not see who or what was aboard. The boat maintained speed, neither drawing ahead nor falling back. It simply rode along in formation, and I could not imagine why. Just before the entrance to Indian Kill where I was about to turn off to the yacht basin, a flap was raised in the side curtain and a hand signaled me to stop. Then the driver revealed himself to be the member I had spoken to at Poughkeepsie. "I forgot to warn you about the markers at the entrance here," he said. "They are a little confusing if you don't know them." And when I came to look at them, they were. But he explained how to follow the markers and then departed at a rate of knots ten miles back to Poughkeepsie with my gratitude still hanging in the air. This occurred on my first day on the Hudson River after leaving New York and was not, I later appreciated, a hospitable fluke but the keynote to New York State inhabitants' reaction to strangers. The natives (loud cheers!) are not hostile. New York State has some marvelous vacation spots, but it is not primarily a resort center. As tourism is not the main trade, a stranger is afforded the kind of hospitality that used to be given automatically to visitors before so many of them lost their traveler's status and became tourists.

New York State is well worth cruising on its own account. The people are so friendly and the scenery is eye-catching and varied, magnificent in places, pastoral in others. The upper part of the state is strangely reminiscent of England (there was a flavor of Stroud in Gloucestershire about some of the towns), which I did not expect, for people were always pointing out to me the differences between the two countries. But in fact, I found a great deal in the northeastern part of my tour that reminded me vividly, both architecturally and scenically, of the British Isles.

From a boatman's point of view New York State is only just short of paradise, and I imagine for those who don't mind winter, it *is* paradise. It is as amphibious as any countryside can get without being entirely under water. It has a foot in the Atlantic Ocean, its head in the Great Lakes and the St. Lawrence River and it is criss-crossed all over by a veritable network of canals, rivers and lakes. A trailer-boatman should have a hard time running out of boating possibilities.

A trip up the Hudson River is impressive from the start, for scenically New York City is only rivaled on the lower reaches by the vertical cliffs of the Palisades across the river. The gentle green mountains farther up have a verdant magnificence of their own. Fascinating Dutch nomenclature, with "kills" for "creeks," bespatters the maps to remind one of the earliest settlers, and one wonders what they made of this rich voluptuous country when they first came to it.

For those who need more than basic scenery there are trimmings. West Point, meticulously neat as becomes a military academy. The "mothball" fleet at Haverstraw, rows and rows of sad silent ships, laid away against an emergency sane people hope will never arise. And there are historical associations a mile high for every inch of the way. But present railway trains intrigued me more than past battles. Living for so long on islands where there aren't any, and in Miami at the end of the line, I had forgotten about railways, and found it quite disconcerting to be overtaken by trains, on both sides of the river. The Hudson River is very wide and tends to dwarf everything, even the mountains. The trains looked like toys, though by European standards they are mastodons.

Albany, the state capital and an inland port, is about

150 miles up the river. I stopped at the Albany Yacht Club for stores, gas and lunch. I also hoped to glean some first hand last minute clarifying information about the *locks*, the threat of which was very close now. I say *threat* because most of the information I had been able to garner had been of the discouraging kind. "You'll never manage alone. How are you going to pass a line down to yourself from a quay forty feet above the boat?" "Watch out for the frightful white water, sink a little boat like yours." "Towboats swing and crush you against the lock walls like an eggshell." That sort of stuff. There were a few who said, "It's a breeze." I was afraid that theirs was the comfort of indifference—they never explained just *how* it would be a breeze. I had no experience of "locking through" except with the two locks at either end of the Dismal Swamp Canal on the Intracoastal Waterway between Miami and New York. But apparently these were kid stuff compared with the commerical locks on the Barge Canals of New York State.

"Don't expect any help from the lock operators," I was warned, and I gained the impression that lock-masters were naturally angry men, impatient and irascible, direct descendants of Bligh and the Red Queen. In the light of experience, some ninety locks later, I am completely at a loss as to how such an impression could have possibly arisen. Without exception, I found all lock operators to be most helpful and very pleasant and to evince an unusual interest and pride in their work. But all I knew at Albany was that there were some thirty locks on the next stretch, between

Troy and Oswego, and that Troy was only a few miles ahead. It was all rather disheartening. And it was raining, too.

But a brief sojourn at the Albany Yacht Club brightened the outlook considerably. A couple on a cabin cruiser, southward bound, had just come through the locks and made light of the experience. They gave me some useful literature on the locks and said, "You'll have no trouble with your little boat." This time I was inclined to be more assured. The steward of the yacht club, accustomed to boats going through the locks all the time, insisted there was really nothing to worry about, and made a couple of fenders — burlap bags stuffed with hay — which he hung fore and aft on the starboard side of the boat. "This'll take care of her," he said, "and you can throw them away when you're through."

They were pretty good fenders, but a little discomposing at times when I entered a lock chamber too fast; the merest brush of the sturdy haybag against the wall would send the boat bouncing across the basin like a rubber ball. Actually the haybags were good for about half a dozen locks, by which time they were waterlogged and weighed a ton. They gave the boat an awful list and put a fearful drag on her, so I abandoned them. By then I had a fairly good grounding in the art of locking and did not need quite such stout physical and moral support. In place of the haybags I hung light Styrofoam fenders, three on either side, fore, amidships and aft. I also led a line on either side from the bow to the cockpit where it was made fast. The boat was then equipped to go either side of the lock as directed by the lockmaster, without my having to change lines and fenders in short order at close quarters. The foam fenders looked fragile, but withstood the wear and tear extremely well (they are still in use at the time of writing) and they were light and inconspicuous to leave in place. Boats traversing the locked waterways do so permanently fendered. On entering the lock small boats like *Gemini* are directed to take a station by one of the vertical ladders that scale the lock walls. Boatmen with skiff-type boats simply hold on to the rungs, but my small boat had a bit more weight and will and needed more direct control. I preferred to slip a bight of the fore-and-aft line (set up specifically for this purpose) over a rung, moving it up and down to the next rung as the water rose or fell. By a judicious pull on the line I could keep the head or stern of the boat from swinging onto the harsh lock walls. In certain conditions this could be quite a task, especially at the bottom of a deep lock where a wind goes mad like a bee in a bottle trying to get out.

A dreamboat called *Scherzo 2½*, belonging to Palmer Myran, conductor of the Michigan City Symphony Orchestra, came into the Albany Yacht Club whilst I was still there. Fulfilling a lifelong ambition, Myran had had the handsome, rugged ketch built in Nova Scotia and now, with a crew of two, was sailing her, on her maiden voyage, home to Lake Michigan. The vertical limit (imposed by certain fixed bridges) for traveling the barge canals is fifteen feet, so the *Scherzo 2½* was brought into Albany Yacht Club to have her masts unstepped. I always meant to ask about the "2½," especially about the "½." Did it represent a past dinghy, I wondered, or had it some musical significance that escaped my mundane mind? But I never got round to inquiring — I was too full of concern for the things to come to think about much else, and most of our encounters after Albany occurred in midstream or in the locks, neither particularly propitious occasions for small talk.

Just before I left the yacht club, the steward there rounded up the local press. This was one for the small-world department, for the reporter was an Englishman. "I remember you," he said, "when you made your trip across the Atlantic." He turned to his photographer and said with a sudden, totally unexpected, nationalistic passion, "She's *famous* in England." The photographer merely looked blank, but my ego, conceited little beast, sailed away to Cloud Nine, and stayed there, smirking, all the way to the Troy Federal Lock.

At Troy the waterways branch; the Hudson River carries on north and the Mohawk River carries the Erie Barge Canal System for the first ninety miles of its long 350-mile trek across the state to Buffalo, on Lake Erie. About halfway, at a point where three rivers meet (called Three Rivers — what else?) the Oswego Canal leads to Lake Ontario, where I was bound eventually.

Traffic is controlled at the locks by lights similar to road traffic signals, red for stop and green for go. When you arrive at a lock you give, according to regulations, "three blasts on the whistle," to let the lockmaster know you're there, and he responds with a light signal. Some locks have loud hailers and tell you what to do.

The lock at Troy is just beyond the turnoff. I got the red light there and lay to to wait for the lock to unload the towboat which it was bringing through from the west. When the towboat emerged and the light turned green I moved to enter, but a giant voice came out of the blue in a startling manner to direct me to "stand by, stand by—let the commercial vessel through." I stood by smartly to allow a sneaky oil tanker, which had been secretly communing with the lock over ship-to-shore and had soundlessly crept up astern of me, to amble by and juggle itself into the lock chamber without, it seemed, an inch to spare on either side. When the clanging and clatter had subsided and the gates were closed, the giant voice came over the air again. "Afraid you'll have to wait awhile, honey," it said.

Commercial vessels, understandably, have right of way over pleasure boats at the locks; but when there is a rush of traffic, pleasure boats are allowed through on every third "go."

There are no charges to pass through any of the New York State locks, which is simply phenomenal in these high-cost days when one is required to pay for the privilege of even *stopping* private transport, in the form of parking a car. But one does need permission to pass through, and this is obtained from the lockmaster at the first lock one enters. The Troy lock, being Federal, hands out its own permits, which are not transferable to the locks on the rest of the system. A new pass is acquired at the next lock, No. 2, three miles further along the line. This is the first of the "Flight," five locks in series with a total lift of 168.8 feet in just over a mile. It is a remarkable engineering feat, a memorable experience and a fine way of getting concentrated lock training. You are no sooner out of one lock than you are into the next, and by the time you've cleared the "Flight" you are lock-happy and ready to take on anything the engineers can think up.

Once you are in the "Flight" there is no escape until you are through. And there is no stopping either, except of course in the normal course of locking through. The lock-keepers at either end of the "Flight" like to collect a flock of boats before starting operations and herd them through the series together. As each batch of boats leaves a lock, the lockmaster phones ahead to the next lock to say so many boats are on the way, and if so many boats don't turn up, out go the St. Bernards.

It was getting late by the time I entered the first of the "Flight" and the lockmaster there suggested his cousin's small-boat dock at Crescent Lake as a suitable stopover for the night. When I eventually got to Crescent Lake, which appeared to be a large and indented swelling of the Mohawk River, it was quite dark, and there was no sign of a boat dock anywhere. A fisherman in an outboard skiff saw me groping about (me and my night-eyes) and came up to see if he could help. He then went several miles out of his way to show me to the lockmaster's cousin's boat dock.

This turned out to be a pleasant outboard fishing camp in a sheltered, overhung inlet where willing hands fussed about tying up the *Gemini* as if she was the *Queen Mary* or the *Yacht Goldenmast.*

11

TO PROTECT banks and revetments in the canals there is a speed limit of 10 m.p.h. It is not easy to cheat, as departures from each lock are phoned ahead to the next, and the lockmaster there knows just exactly how long it takes to cover the distance between. However, the official attitude towards outboards in this respect seems to be fairly flexible. It appears to be recognized that an outboard at 10 m.p.h. is likely to raise a far more damaging wash than it would going faster on plane, and it is the wash that is of concern rather than the speed itself. I made my arrivals at and departures from the locks in a circumspect manner at about 6 m.p.h., and then when conditions were suitable, planed at about 20 m.p.h. Both speeds leave a negligible wake, and no one complained (though one lockmaster was taken by surprise: "Where did *you* spring from?").

The locks are electrically operated and in good shape. They have undergone considerable reconstruction since the system was completed in 1825. When one considers the equipment available in those days, the vision and tenacity needed to put through the project must have been enormous. No. 17 is a very modern lock. It has the highest single lift in the system, making a hoist of 40 feet, and it has smooth steel-lined walls against which one's boat glides silkily on the journey up or down. Instead of the usual miter-gates, it has a drop gate like a portcullis. But the lock is red-ringed in my memory because the lock-master there made an unusual utterance. He said, "You must have been around boats a long time, the way you handle that one." He said it casually, *en passant*, without a note of condescension. It is the rarest thing for a man to compliment a woman to her face on her conduct of an activity generally regarded as being in the masculine field. Though why modern boating, which requires nothing in the way of physical strength, is regarded thus, it is hard to imagine. But it is. Especially in America where masculine and feminine activities are curiously but rigidly defined. The squaw complex is very strong and one of the things American women *don't* do is to take the initiative outdoors. But if by any chance a female shows a propensity to excel in anything outside the closed circuit of the woman's sphere, she is strongly advised by the lonely-hearts column to watch it, kid, keep those brains and biceps under cover, there's masculinity at stake. But with masculinity that delicate, who wants it, for Pete's sake? Surely there is only one criterion of the masculine and feminine state, one difference? —and as the French say, *vive la*—the rest is up to the individual, and the species is infinitely variable.

When I first came to the States, I was absolutely enchanted by the outspoken, extrovert admiration of the American male. (The best you can get from an Englishman is a quick twitch of the tie, and you've got to be alert to catch it.) Then I realized it wasn't for me at all, it was for the *concept* of women. For in America, women aren't looked on as people. They are symbols for sex, and the ideal woman is popularly portrayed as a sexy half-wit. There is nothing to actually stop a woman from becoming president of a bank, a nuclear physicist or an engineer. In fact, many of them do, but they are performing seals. A woman can be a female Einstein, but if she isn't married she's a flop. For all the talk, in western culture, there is still only one way for a woman to attain universal acceptance and acclaim as a person in her own right, and that is to become a successful high-class tart.

However, perhaps the lockmaster's singular remark may be a sign of a breakthrough, and American women may yet achieve people status. As a matter of fact I caught a glimpse of one who had, operating a gas dock at Sylvan Beach on the eastern side of Lake Oneida. The lake is twenty miles long and one of those bodies of water with a direful reputation. "Rough! Wait'll you cross Lake Oneida. Is she *rough!* Even the towboats can't make it sometimes." It would appear the reputation is not unfounded, and advice to get a weather check before crossing the lake is meant to be taken seriously. A lockmaster on the eastern side of the lake suggested I should stop at the Gulf Dock in Sylvan Beach for this. "It is run by a woman," he said, "a fine, interesting woman, you'll enjoy meeting her, and she knows all about the lake." She was a pretty woman, direct and very efficient. She refueled the tanks, and brought ice and a weather report down to the boat almost as quickly as it takes to write. It was a blustery, unpromising morning. "But it is going to get worse," she warned. "If you want to cross the lake today you had better go now. It is blowing twenty m.p.h. right now and it'll be rough for the first seven miles, then you'll be in the lee and it will be all right."

And so it was. I could see by the way the lake behaved it might be a very unpleasant place when the wind really began to blow.

Traveling the canals is a wonderful way to see the state. It cannot help but be leisurely and therefore soothing. The scenery is pleasantly pastoral, and the small towns one passes through are old-world in appearance and easygoing in atmosphere. There was surprisingly little traffic and I went through most of the locks alone, secretly a little embarrassed at causing so much machinery to be put in motion for so small a boat. But there was never a dark look. Fuel pumps are few and far between, but not too far, and where there are none for boats a garage will usually oblige. At the town of Little Falls, to which one comes after passing through the portcullis of No. 17 lock, there is an enterprising service station proprietor called Johnnie, a curly-haired Italian who snakes the nozzle of a gasoline pipe through the revetment railings for you to fill your tanks and swings a ladder over the rails for you to go ashore, all the while engaging you with a bubbling account of Johnnie, his immigration, life and times.

There is a paucity of marinas too on the barge canals, but there are public wharves in the center of every town where one can tie up free of charge. Standpipes for water are usually available and a telephone booth nearby.

The landings are usually just the right height for small boats, there are no tides to fret about and of course there is perfect protection. So what more could one want? On the canals it is easier to stop and tie up a boat than it is to park a car in the towns. There was one exception, at Rome (I love the crazy mixed-up geography in the States). Here landing was complicated by a baulk of timber, a sturdy 10″ x 12″, running the length of the quay wall, about 3 feet below the top and 2 feet away from it (figures approximate; they seemed much worse). Bollards were placed several yards back from the edge of the quay. This was a big-ship-type operation, not a small-boat landing at all. Taking the lines ashore to the bollards was a perilous matter, but the return journey was even worse: One was jumping the gap downhill, and the ten-inch beam, level with *Gemini*'s cabin-top, didn't seem nearly enough to land on. It made one think twice about going ashore, but Rome was a strategic place to stop for the night and there was nowhere else to tie up.

Four pleasure boats moored there that night, which was most unusual. There was the *Scherzo 2½*, another sailboat, a cruiser and *Gemini* and we took up almost the whole length of the wharf.

About midnight I was awakened by the most fearful clamor. Bells clanging, engines throbbing, propellers threshing, a staccato bellowing of orders, and a searchlight playing about like sheet lightning. I looked out and saw an oil barge bent on coming alongside the wharf. Obviously there would be no room for us if he did. It was raining. And we were there first.

"They're not supposed . . ." hollered the skipper. "Get them *out of there!*" Two men, loudly protesting, were somehow put ashore to roust us out. They stumped up and down the quay shouting, "Ho yacht, ho yacht, *Ho Yacht!*" and the searchlight shone on each of us in turn, but the thought of dancing about that trick landing in the dark and rain was too much. No one moved a muscle — a concerted reaction as if it had been mutually agreed upon beforehand. The four boats lay darkened by the dock, lifeless, inert, and unassailably obdurate. The skipper and the two men ashore had a fascinating altercation. The skipper favored some positive action, but the men were against this because in the event of a mistake they'd be the ones to be clobbered. Meantime the barge backed and filled, jilling irritably about the canal. It was quite impossible for anyone to have slept through the racket, it was completely out of character that *no one* evinced the slightest curiosity, and it was highly unlikely that the entire crews of all four boats should still be out on the town (after midnight — in a small town like Rome, N.Y.?). But we weren't to be smoked out. Finally, after failing to call our bluff, the tanker crew were forced to juggle a heavy hose ashore by remote control. Judging by the sound effects, this must have been quite an operation. Unfortunately it took place outside my field of vision, and under the circumstances I did not feel it was politic to go out into the cockpit to watch. When the job was done, the hose was juggled back aboard, and the tanker went away, furiously stamping the water with its propellers and giving a ponderous flirt of its stern, narrowly missing the obstructive boats and giving the uncooperative crews fits.

Next morning I met Palmer Myran on *Scherzo 2½* in a lock and said, "Hey, how about all that jazz last night?"

"Yes," he said, looking somewhat abashed, "we all lay low. Wasn't it awful?"

iii

OSWEGO belongs in my list of implausible place names along with Oshkosh, Tomsk, Kalamazoo and Auchtermuchty, all of which sound as if they had been made up on the spur of the moment in a parlor game. However, there is nothing implausible about the town of Oswego as it looks out across the great Lake Ontario from the end of the Oswego Canal, a twenty-four-mile offshoot from the Erie Waterway. It is a sound little town cut out of the rock, with an historic foursquare fort, sturdy foursquare architecture, and large shady trees. The canal cleaves the center of town, stepping down to lake level by two locks, adding character to an already picturesque scene.

Commercial traffic on the canal is not so heavy; the bulk of water-borne freight is taken along the main road of the Erie Canal to Buffalo. But a considerable and increasing amount of pleasure boating passes to and fro, since Oswego is a strategic point for cruising the eastern end of Lake Ontario, the St. Lawrence and the eastern waterways of the Province of Ontario, Canada. In spite of this and the fact that it borders on the lake, Oswego is not a resort town. It has other, more substantial affairs to attend to, and lives a natural existence in which growth and decay balance one another and the atmosphere is relaxed. With enough time and space around them, the townsfolk are warmhearted without any of that repellent professional charm-school bonhomie that so often passes for friendliness in places where business is boomtown, seasonal or transient.

Trenton was the goal I was aiming for on the Canadian side of Lake Ontario, and I stopped at Oswego to case the lake. It is nearly two hundred miles long from east to west — by no means the biggest of the Great Lakes, but big enough to be taken seriously. The crossing I was to make entailed nearly sixty miles of open water, and the fact that it was drinking water did not make it any less potentially formidable.

No. 7, the upper lock in Oswego, doubles as a marina. There is no dockage for pleasure boats in the town, but the lay-by on the east side of the lock makes an excellent place to tie up. It is handy for stores and perfectly sheltered. There were nine boats there when I arrived, and the night before there had been twenty-two. Much of the popularity of the place was due to the lockmaster, Wesley Smith, who not only made the boatmen welcome, but went out of his way to make their stay comfortable and pleasant. No host could care more for a guest. A mere mention of something you wanted or wanted to know and Wesley Smith was on the phone, ordering or inquiring, and before you knew what was what, there it was, your requirement or your answer. Anyone who starts a marina in Oswego has his work cut out to keep up to the standard set by Wesley's private yacht basin at No. 7 lock.

Three things I wanted at Oswego. Charts for the landfall at Presqu'ile Point near Trenton. Information about the wandering compass variation. And good weather.

Well, there isn't much one can do about good weather but wait for good weather reports, and in spite of almost feverish cooperation from the lockmaster and the townsfolk I could get neither the charts nor the information I wanted.

There are certain places in Lake Ontario and in parts of other Great Lakes where the variation is erratic and the compass goes mad and lies like crazy. And the condition is apparently elusive, so that you cannot say that the variation at this point is thus and thus. It is here today and gone somewhere else tomorrow with a greater or lesser error.

"You want to watch it," said the skipper of a small cruiser bound for the St. Lawrence, "it can sure throw you off. I know a guy who got caught in one of these variation hassles and followed his compass round in circles until he ran out of gas in the middle of the lake, and it was ten hours before someone picked him up and towed him in."

"But couldn't he tell he was off course by the sun — or that he was going round in circles by his wake?"

"There was a thick fog. Came down after he'd set out. You want to watch that too."

I wasn't sure whether he was pulling my leg. There seems little doubt that erratic compass variations exist in these parts, but I was unable to obtain any specific details. Even a visit to the local Coast Guard Station drew a blank. The officers there regarded me sternly when I questioned them, and pointed out that the Canadian side of the lake was outside their jurisdiction, and that they knew of no variation variables in *their* waters (one felt they wouldn't allow it). There was nothing to be done, as far as I could see, but "watch it" like the man said.

Canadian charts were unobtainable in Oswego, except for Kingston, at the headwaters of the St. Lawrence and 70 miles east of Trenton, where I wanted to be.

"So why not go to Kingston?" suggested the cruiser skipper when I wailed slightly. "It's a nice place, and you can get all the charts you want there. And it's a lovely trip from Kingston to Trenton through the Bay of Quinte."

Why not? I thought. Charts are eyes for a boat. Better go where I can see.

So at the first fair weather report, three days after arriving in Oswego, I set out for Canada, with Kingston as my port.

"Fair" was a comparative term. The local weather bureau, with a watch literally on the lake, gave immediate conditions as calm with one mile visibility, but warned of a strong southwest wind to come later in the morning. I thought I could make it across before anything started. The visibility was down to half a mile by the time I was through the locks and out on the lake, and a huge swell was rolling up from the southwest. It wasn't long before the wind to match it arrived. Early, as if it had been waiting in ambush.

Gemini bounded along like a startled stag. She leapt off the crests of the quartering waves, landed in the troughs with a jolt and a splash, and roared up to the top of the next wave to take off again. It was a hard way of traveling, and could have been eased a lot by slower going, but I was anxious to get as far as possible across the lake before the weather got really bad. I just about made it, although *Gemini* was down to a brisk crawl at the end.

There was a little compass disturbance, a tendency to put the boat *west* of her course, which in view of the strong sou'westerly wind blowing was unlikely to be caused by drift. It could, however, have been deviation caused by electrical equipment installed in New York.

Visibility did not improve very much despite the wind, and my first view of Canada was through the mist, darkly. It was cold and all rather dispiriting, so when I came to the Kingston Yacht Club, which lies a mile or two west of the town, I turned into the yacht basin, a crowded, jumbled little harbor, picturesque in a dilapidated sort of way, affording far more shelter than seems possible. Seen from the water, it appears to be wide open to all winds except those from the north.

I taxied in through the narrow entrance and attached myself to the gas dock, thinking I could refuel, find out about Customs and where to stay, and take a breather.

Kingston Yacht Club is one of the oldest yacht clubs in the country and absolutely devoted to sail. It is questionable whether the members even realize there are any other kinds of boats. Nonetheless the steward, after refueling *Gemini*, said in response to my inquiry regarding somewhere to tie up, "I'll find a space for you here." And what is more, he arranged for me to use the club facilities, which almost amounted to a cattleman bringing a shepherd home to the ranch; and it's a wonder he was allowed to get away with it.

Clearing Customs into Canada was an agreeable procedure, singularly free from red tape. I called up first from the club to say I had arrived, and then walked a mile or so into town to fill out the forms.

I didn't *have* to walk, but I *like* walking and firmly believe you can see a place better on foot than from the inside of a comparatively fast-moving vehicle. There is a better chance of seeing the differences and clearing up some of the inevitable misconceptions. If you haven't the time to live amongst the people, you should at least walk amongst them. One of the first reactions I always have on my first visit to a country is of surprise at how *little* we know of our neighbors. How scant is our general knowledge of other lives, and how many and extraordinary are the misconceptions we cherish.

Most English people believe that Canada is a sparse U.S.A. with Christmas trees. And that Canadians are slightly underprivileged U.S. citizens. To the English, American and Canadian accents are as indistinguishable as Cockney and Yorkshire accents are to Americans and Canadians. A type of tone-deafness each finds incomprehensible in the other. My first impression of Canada, through Kingston, was how *un*like the States it was, and how similar it was to Britain in atmosphere. I felt that I had in effect crossed the ocean and not the lake. For instance, if you were to stop in the main street of Oswego and look about you perplexed, someone would be sure to ask if he could help. "Looking for something, ma'am?" If you stopped in downtown Kingston and looked perplexed you might stand there till Doomsday before anyone offered to assist. In Kingston they figure you have a perfect right to look perplexed if you want to, and it would be an intrusion on your privacy to butt in before being asked. As soon as I realized that the Canadians, at least in Ontario, suffer from the almost pathological reserve that afflicts the British, I understood the overwhelmingly extravagant ardor with which I was greeted by an American yacht in the Kingston approaches. *Gemini* of course was flying the American flag, and at the sight of it everyone aboard the yacht rushed to the side, creating quite a ballast situation, and waved with such hysterical abandon as to almost imperil the stability of their boat. It puzzled me at the time, but now I figure they were probably on their first visit and, unaware of the Ontarian restraint in which privacy is prized above pearls, thought they must have suddenly become invisible and were checking up.

Kingston has an old-fashioned dignity. The buildings are handsome in the best Victorian manner without being baroque and are solid enough to withstand a siege. It is a well-timbered town. Huge trees with tall straight trunks smooth as columns line the sidewalks, their branches stretching out to make a canopy over the road. Three-story basement houses, semidetached, vast Siamese twins of brick and stone, ivy-covered and impregnable, dominate the residential scene. Pillar-boxes, rotund and British, stand at street corners for mailing letters. Traffic slides by noiselessly. Kingston is a quiet town. Sedate. So I was surprised — and delighted — to come on a market spang in the middle of an open square near the docks and the Customs house. And a roistering rowdy market, flaunting a mad jumble of wares, edible, textile, domestic and farm, apples, oranges, marrows, carrots, cabbages, tomatoes, black aubergines, white eggs, chickens, chairs, and rainbow bolts of cloth under striped awnings and gay umbrellas, about which vendors and buyers were loud in contrapuntal debate.

Shadows are so much part of our lives today it is not always easy to recognize substance at first glance. My immediate reaction to the market was mild. Television show? No, no cameras. Movie set? No, no cameras. An advertisement? Too big, no glamour girls. Chamber of Commerce gag to stupefy tourists and wrest the dough from them? No, far too lively. It just had to be the real thing. An honest-to-goodness all-out haggle of a market, genuine, fundamental and down to earth, bright and gay, dusty and lusty, and look, Ma, no Cellophane.

The casual approach to hygiene with regard to food continues out of the market square and into the shops, most of which display their wares — animal, vegetable and mineral — on the sidewalk so at least there'll be no danger of your walking into the wrong shop. The Customs officer advised me to go to a grocery store for my charts, which seemed a little odd, and I felt foolish standing in the middle of an undoubted aromatic and spicy grocery emporium asking for charts. But the white-aproned assistant merely reached up to a shelf and produced a chart for the Bay of Quinte along with some excellent cheese, as if it were perfectly normal to stock such unlikely commodities together.

I landed in Canada on August 15th and I was getting worried. Summer was almost over and I was not yet at the "top" of my climb north. In two months the Trent-Severn Waterway would be officially closed, and if I didn't get a move on there was a good chance of being caught in the trap of winter. What made me even more anxious to get rolling was that Bert was taking a vacation at the beginning of September and driving up to meet me. The less distance he had to drive the more time we would have together. It was unanimously agreed that telephones were no substitute for marriage. I was, as usual—and in spite of a fast boat—making slower progress than anticipated. There are so many things to slow one down: the need to stop for stores, for charts, for information, to write, to sketch, to take pictures, and simply to rest, to say nothing of the limitations imposed by weather—or locks. But now I felt I *must* get on, come what might. And what came of course was a howling headwind.

I could go and spend a lot of fuel and energy getting nowhere in particular or wait for better weather. Whilst I was panther-prowling the dock in indecision, Hilton Lapun, the yacht club steward, made a counter-suggestion. "My friends and I are going for a picnic by a lake," he said in his quiet courteous manner. "Would you care to join us?"

This is another reason for allowing non-traveling days to almost equal traveling days in a cruise, and a good one.

Hilton's friends, Jim and Betty Braithwaite and their rollicking family of four kids, were just the right cast for a proper picnic scene, and the setting by a lake, not the Great Lake, but one of those lovely little tree-girt gems with which Ontario is so liberally supplied.

Betty's surname, coloring and accent made me certain that the Braithwaites were Scottish, recently immigrated, but they assured me they were firmly entrenched Canadians from way back. Later I was to discover that many Ontarians speak with a Scottish accent, a very pronounced one employing all the Scottish vocal mannerisms. There is not an immediate Scottish background to account for this and the people I spoke to were not in the least aware of their accent being Scots. Yet an unmistakable Scottish atmosphere pervades, increasing as one goes farther north and west, and as the country grows wilder one can detect a certain fey quality — and some of the lawlessness too — that one finds amongst the Highlanders. Even the terrain has such a Scottish look about it in places that there were moments when I wondered if *Gemini* wasn't some sort of time-machine taking me back to the years I spent in the Highlands.

After the picnic, Jim, who was driving, insisted on taking us for a ride so that I could see some of the country. Considering that he had some fantastic distance like seventy miles to drive every day to work, this was uncommonly hospitable of him. We drove through bald hummocky districts where rocks showed like bones through the thin fabric of the earth and stunted trees grew in stubborn tufts on small round hills, and then we drove through exquisite little valleys where the vegetation was almost tropical in the luxuriance of its growth. Pride in local beauty made Jim pile up the miles in an effort to show me the best of the Rideau Canal, a well-known and popular cruising ground, and he and Hilton argued the merits of the various locks, the local showplaces. We stopped to look at two of them. They were of special interest to me, apart from their undeniable loveliness, as they gave some idea of what to expect on the Trent Waterways to come — tomorrow, I hoped.

But tomorrow only brought more bad weather and it wasn't until the day after that I was heading down the North Channel for the Bay of Quinte, Trenton and the beginning of the Trent-Severn Valley Canal System.

It was a lovely day, well worth waiting for, and by late afternoon I was in Trenton, suffering from such a mental surfeit of rolling, parklike, bland and beautiful scenery that all I could remember of the seventy-mile run through the Bay of Quinte was the impudent-looking little boat-shaped light buoys which marked the channels.

I stopped at the public wharf for charts but the dockmaster there told me I would have to get them at the first lock; then he asked me to sign a register with such a bright expectant look on his face I felt bound to reward him, though for what was not quite clear. A small boy then begged a ride to the first lock, about a mile up the river, and upon our arrival pressed into my hand a card advertising a hamburger stand in Times Square, New York City. Of course he had to be rewarded too, whereupon he disembarked and headed straight back to the town (and another boat?). Waiting to go through the lock were three sailors, taking a busman's holiday with an outboard and doing their best to lighten ship by drinking their cargo of beer, quietly but with conscientious effort.

I got my charts from the lockmaster, and a "let-pass," the permit for which there is no charge but without which one cannot cruise the Trent, and then as I followed the Navy's wake of empty beer cans through the lock, I thought sourly that the Trent Waterways showed all the earmarks of a first-class tourist trap. Gaudy gift shops, Indian artifacts, puerile postcards — here I come!

IV

IF EVER I had a wrong impression, that was it. Far from being a tourist trap, the Trent country in Ontario is still unspoilt and innocent in spite of being a vacation area and having a history of long and bitter exploitation.

The Trent-Severn Valley Waterway is a series of lakes and rivers linked by canals and locks to connect the Lake Ontario and Lake Huron districts. The Waterway is 240 miles long and there are 43 locks and two marine railways to obviate the vast portage that explorer Champlain and the native Indians had to put up with. Construction of the Waterway was begun in a lumber boom in 1833. Canals and locks were dug and built where they would most facilitate the removal of timber. Pretty effectively, too, because long, *long* before the Waterway system was finished, the forests were. The lumbermen had cleared the area and gone. Settlers moved in and for a while were responsible for some activity on the waters, but greedy farming continued the depredation so enthusiastically begun by the lumbermen until at last erosion drove the settlers away. Roads and railways took what little traffic remained and in 1918 the government gave up the project and the last two locks that would have completed the system were never built. Instead, two makeshift marine railways were erected.

One would expect a vista of barren lands, the unwilling operation of tumble-down locks by dispirited lock-keepers and a pervading atmosphere of defeat and dissolution, but one finds scenery of unsurpassable beauty in an atmosphere of lighthearted insouciance, the sort of cheerful idiocy that delights one so in Ireland where logic masquerades as folly and reason goes mad.

Pilotage on the lakes, for instance. Lakes are legion and the channels are devious and beset by rocks, reefs, stumps, snags and even in one place—Rice Lake—a submerged railway. In the middle of Stony Lake, which is perfectly lovely but, as one might gather, chocka-block with islands, islets, rocks, reefs and bars, I stopped the boat and through binoculars tried to make sense of the channel which had petered out in a rock-bound pool. The channel bore off to the left somewhere, but for the life of me I could not see where. A pecked line plainly indicated the passage on the chart; but pecked lines do not show on the water, and in this instance the rocks and islands of the lake did not show on the chart—at least not with sufficient detail to identify them. The Trent Waterways have not been fully surveyed; consequently the charts of that area are often grievously lacking in pertinent information. Slender stakes marked the channel, but Stony is a popular resort lake, and channels are being made and staked out all the time, apparently without any regard to channels and marks already existing. Thus a network of channels running athwart, around and parallel to one another creates a forest of stakes in some places and a dearth of them in others. The net result towards directional navigation is nil. There was a dearth of them right then. The islands are mainly small but high and rocky, topped with thick growths of scrub and pine, and they effectively blocked my view. Round which one of them went the channel, I wondered. There was absolutely no indication.

Although most of the islands are barely as big as the average building lot there are hardly any without a summer home nestling unobtrusively in the trees, and some of the houses are remarkably ambitious, considering the problems entailed in building on a practically unapproachable island in an almost unnavigable lake. There was a balconied two-storied house on an island not far from where I was stalled, debating the next move, and a man in pajamas came out onto the balcony, yawning and stretching, for his early morning gaze on the lake. Ah-hah, I thought, on-the-spot information, and taxied towards him through the round-backed rocks, feeling my way delicately because of a suspicion that rocks share with icebergs the peculiarity of having nine-tenths and all the danger submerged. Within loud conversational distance I stopped the motors and asked the way to Burleigh, the next lock along the line, with a town and well-known falls to boot, and therefore an obvious place to inquire about. Better than "How do I get outa here?"

"Burleigh? Burleigh Falls?" The man came to the edge of the balcony to verify this and leaned over the rail. "It's over there," and he pointed in the direction I knew I ought to take but for the rocks and islands in the way.

"Yes," I said, "but how?"

"How?" He looked rather pointedly at the boat and I thought, well, the man's only just got up, and then he said, "The channel's marked, you can't miss it."

"I have missed it, where do I find it from here?"

He walked to the far end of the balcony and leaned over: "You see that island with a green-roofed house on it?"

By standing on the cabin top I could just see the roof-top over the intervening islands.

"Go up to that island and turn left there. You'll see a day-mark, a white board, in the trees on an island about half a mile ahead. That'll lead you to the main channel and Burleigh."

That's fine, I thought, but how to get to the green roof?

"What about all these rocks?" I said.

"What about them," said the man yawning. "You can see them, can't you?"

The locks are built to accommodate vessels up to 121 feet in length with a maximum beam of 21 feet, but the marine railways cannot handle anything bigger than a fifty-footer — if it isn't any wider than 13½ feet. If you drove a 51-foot boat up from Trenton you would never make it to Georgian Bay, because the first marine railway would stop you. As if you hadn't gone crazy long before that. The official size limits for a vessel traversing the Trent are highly optimistic. To enjoy the Waterway it must be traveled in a small boat. The smooth walls of some of the locks may delude one into believing they are less than a hundred years old, but their operational methods never would. To open the massive miter gates, the lock operator, and anyone he can persuade to help him, has to push a turn bar round and round like an ox treading out corn, a long, laborious, back-breaking job. Being sensible men, lock-tenders do not open more than one of the double gates unless it is absolutely necessary, and that one gate they will open only wide enough to enable a boat to sidle round. So when the wind and current play up, as they often do, it takes some nice maneuvering to enter a lock and make a landing by the wall as indicated by the lockmaster. Since bridges are also only opened by the ox trick and bridge-tenders are also sensible men, a bridge won't be opened for a boat unless the operator is absolutely sure (and you can bet he knows to an eighth of an inch) that the boat won't clear it closed. If he does open the bridge he is unlikely to open it all the way, and a half open swing bridge with a fast running stream calls for some more of that fancy boat handling. There are 43 locks and at least as many low-level bridges on the Trent Waterways. What with these to tax his skill and the narrow, shallow, ill-defined channels with sharp turns in them to keep him guessing, a big boat skipper has his hands (if not his heart) full cruising the Trent.

Gemini was small and agile and waltzed round the lock gates and snaked under the low bridges with no trouble at all. She was also comparatively easy to handle during the locking process. In the Trent locks one does not hold on to the wall ladders as in the Erie locks: there are chains hanging down the walls for this purpose. The chains are loose-footed and rather hard on the topsides, though I found that plastering the vulnerable spots with plastic tape gave a measure of protection. I also discovered it was important to see that the chain fell outside the cockpit on a rising lock. There is a tendency for it to fall inside, and twenty or so feet of three-quarter-inch chain is quite a weight.

Not all the locks on the Trent are venerable antiques. Two of them are very elegant antiques, and one of these at least claims a world record. This is the Peterborough lift lock in the heart of the town of Peterborough, the largest town one passes through on the Waterway. The lock, with its 65-foot rise, makes the highest single lift in the world and a bid for fame. It is a handsome, imposing structure and operated in an entirely different manner from the ordinary run-of-the-mill locks. The lock chambers are like huge oblong boxes, giant shoe boxes without the lid. An end gate is lowered under the water for boats to pass over and enter into the lock chamber. After the gates have been closed and everything is ready, the whole shooting match, box, boats, water and all, rides slowly and with great dignity up to the tree tops, or down, as the case may be. The operation is hydraulic. There are two of these boxes, counterbalancing one another. Water is flooded into the upper chamber until it outweighs the lower one, then down it comes and up goes the other (don't look at me, that's the way I understand it). Anyway, it gives the smoothest boat ride, in or out of a lock.

The other lift lock is several miles further on at Kirkfield, at the top of the climb from Trenton, and from there the going is downhill and downstream the rest of the way to Georgian Bay. The channel markers, which up to now have been set for upstream pilotage, red on the right, switch to red on the left for downstream pilotage. Which is reasonable of course, but not so easy to remember.

At Kirkfield I made a 49-foot ride down from the tree tops into the valley below, and after the descent Don Smith, who runs the lock with a crew of two and shares with them the anthropomorphic pride in it that sailors often have for their ships, offered to show me round. We went underneath the boxes, where there is a fantastic plumber's nightmare of piping, a labyrinthine tangle of pipes, joints and cocks to let water in, out, up, down and round in order to move the lock chambers and lift little boats over the falls. Don Smith explained enthusiastically how it all worked, which seemed perfectly clear at the time, but too complicated for my pinbrain to retain except for one obvious statement. "It is all worked by water," he said, adding impressively, "There's nothing electrical here but the lighting." But Smith and his henchmen are very frustrated. The Peterborough lift locks, with their jaunty red and white facings and convenient city location, draw the crowds. The Kirkfield locks are not faced. Theirs is the skeletal beauty of deciduous trees in winter which for many equals full bloom, but they are far out in the lonely countryside and no one drives out to see their wonders. "Now if this was in the States," lamented Don Smith, "it would be written up in all the magazines and people would be coming from all over the country to see it."

Not many people go to look at the marine railways either, and they are interesting too, though probably more fun to ride than to watch. They surprised me, though I am not sure what I expected — certainly nothing so long or so steep as they are. The drop at Swift Rapids is 47 feet and at Big Chute 58 feet and the ride down them is as good as a run on a roller coaster. A small cruiser was coming up when I arrived at Swift Rapids, the first of the two railways going north, and I watched with some awe as it trundled up the long steep hill. No one but the skipper is allowed to stay aboard during transportation. When it came to my turn, according to instructions, I drove *Gemini* on to the semi-submerged cradle until she ran aground, as it were, and heeled over. I cut the motors — but not the thudding of my foolish heart which works up a lather over the simplest of new experiences. The attendant then seized the bow line, leapt aboard the cradle, nonchalantly flung a loop of the line round a stanchion, nodded to the powerhouse and we were off. We crawled up a short steep incline first, creaking and rattling with apparently enormous effort, just the way a roller coaster car pants up the big dip. Then with a jerk the cradle went over the top, lurching skywards in the authentic manner, hung suspended for a microsecond and then took off lickety-split down the slope to land with a splendid shower of spray in the water.

The marine railways, like the Kirkfield lift locks, are way out in the bush, so I suppose it is not really surprising that they don't have many sight-seers. But they are the only lock-type places on the Trent that aren't crowded with visitors. Most of the locks, situated by falls and invariably noted beauty spots, are by way of being gay social centers where people, local and holiday inhabitants and passing travelers, collect to fish, swim, gossip and watch the boats go by. Many lock operators live right by the locks, where they landscape the surroundings, creating lawns and gardens, and act as genial hosts, M.C.'s and general dispensers of news. Far from being soured by what might be considered as onerous work for the benefit of other people's pleasure, the lock-tenders take great pride in both their work and efficiency and they are unfailingly courteous to boatmen.

"There is another boat following you. Would you mind waiting a few minutes for him?" I was asked at one lock. Regrettably, one expects a government official to say either "You'll have to wait" or nothing at all, and just keep you waiting. Of course I didn't mind waiting, but in a few minutes the lockmaster was back again. "Come on," he said, "I'll let you through. That other boat won't be here for half an hour yet." He insisted on locking me through rather than keep me waiting, yet by the time he would be through doing this the other boat would have arrived and immediately he would have to go through the whole performance again. The

"Welcome" sign in the No. 9 lock approaches means what it says and stands for all the locks.

Surprises await you on the Trent. A tame raccoon came bubbling along the quay at one lock to meet me as it met all the boats, hamming it up for rewards and photographs. And another time I met a gorgeous golden family, young parents of two small children, miniature replicas of themselves, who, with a magnificent disregard for the usually prized outer trappings, transcended their worn and faded swim suits and looked as though they had just stepped down from Olympus for a day's slumming amongst the mortals. They asked me to join them for lunch and we picnicked under the trees on the river bank. The talk may have been good — the wine certainly was — but conversation was unnecessary with such people to look at. They caused me to revise my concept of tourists for quite a while.

The Trent is so lovely that "discovery" in due course is inevitable. A thought that saddens its present admirers, for then the authorities will feel impelled to modernize the system, a process that is likely to remove much of the charm and all of the challenge. At present there are not many boatyards and marinas along the Waterway, but there are enough, and with the excellent tie-ups at the quays in every lock approach, and at the wharves in every town center, who wants more?

At Campbellford I was fascinated to discover a further and somewhat unusual example of the Scottish influence in Ontario. The Scots, of course, are world-renowned for their thriftiness and general reluctance to bang a saxpence. In Campbellford this was startlingly exemplified in a rest room where the toilet roll was padlocked to its fitting on the wall.

Peterborough, the home of the glamorous lift lock and the biggest, busiest town on the Waterway, lies about a third of the way along it. This section of the system is the Otonobee River, and as it flows through the town it broadens out just before the lift lock into Little Lake. There are docks there for small boats, charmingly sited in a parklike setting but, in the crazy Trent tradition, hard by a slaughterhouse which takes some of the enchantment out of the view. Otherwise the town is a pleasant mixture of the conservative — stalwart old buildings, leafy avenues, an occasional horse-drawn delivery van clopping along — and the up-and-coming pastel subdivisions, shopping centers and industry. It is also the home of Canada's Outboard Marine, where Evinrude motors are manufactured. When I was on board the *Chanticleer*, Ralph Evinrude had said, "Be sure and call the Neals when you get to Peterborough." Clarence Neal was the president of Outboard Marine there. I'm not much of a name-dropper and too shy to be a name-grabber; and if, in these days when everyone is pushing a wheelbarrow for promotion, I pranced in on Mr. Neal saying, "Look what *I'm* doing with two of your-type motors!" I could imagine him thinking to himself, "Oh, my God, here comes another one." On the other hand, it did not seem polite to drive through Peterborough without saying how d'you do. Lese majesty. Like skipping the book at Government House. So tentatively, a day's run from Peterborough, I put a call through to Clarence

Neal, thereby unwittingly letting myself in for some of the most delightful red-carpet treatment it has been my good fortune to enjoy. Three days I dallied in Peterborough, house guest of Clarence and Kay Neal at their farm in the country, being made to feel at home and as if I had known them all my life. It takes something special in the way of hospitality to engender this on first meeting. Members of the firm, whose business it was to look after visiting firemen, had the same happy knack, so that I left Peterborough with the glow one has after being thoroughly spoilt.

No waterway is complete without its man-eating lake and the one on the Trent is Simcoe, near the Georgian Bay end of the system. As usual, I was inundated with warnings of the terrible conditions the lake could whip up at a moment's notice and regaled with countless tales of deep-sea mariners who had had some of them and quoth "Nevermore!" It was quiescent enough the morning I crossed, though a surge came into the canal that leads into the lake with such force that the backwash made a furious pyramidal turmoil in the water. A skiff came off the lake as I was going down the canal, and its wan-looking occupants warned me: "Watch it. It's sure kicking up today out there." But it wasn't for me. *Gemini* romped across in good order at 22 m.p.h. and my only complaint was that it was too foggy to see the view. And the scenery is something one should not miss on the Trent. There are all kinds, from simple pastoral views to rock-bound magnificence, and they are dramatically laid out for the best effect. The landscape starts quietly at the Trenton end of the Waterway wearing a peaceful rural manner, but gradually it grows more spectacular until by the time you've reached the marine railways the glories are coming at you thick and fast. Deep blue pools of cloud reflections, precipitous walls of red rock, serried rows of pine, dark barbed arrows pointing at the sky. Then before you can catch your breath the vista falls flat on its face in a clutter of billboards and gaudy gew-gaws in the little town at the end of the line, Port Severn, as garish and out of place as a juke box in the Louvre.

The Trent-Severn Valley Waterway ended as it began for me, in disguise.

PART THREE

Lakes

⚓

𝕿
i

THE wonderland, storybook quality that pervades the Trent Waterways persists into Georgian Bay, although there it is of sterner stuff. The Trent has a serenity about it even in its most rugged moments. It belongs to the land, where man is at home. But Georgian Bay is more like the sea, where man is not at home, only temporarily on it by a courtesy that is often quickly revoked. I found it very hard to believe that Georgian Bay was an inlet off a lake. It looked like the sea and behaved like the sea and gave one the same feeling of its being a sleeping tiger, beautiful, unpredictable and dangerous. It was extraordinary to see fresh-water fish idling round barnacle-free pilings, and the lack of salt in the spray was quite shocking. I had not felt this way about Lake Ontario, which is also big and can certainly be rough enough to look sealike, because there the shores are such as one might expect to find round a lake; but the shores on Georgian Bay are seashores, and wild northern seashores at that.

It was baffling, but I could not go so far as the Yorkshire woman I met with her husband in one of the snug little harbors with which the bay abounds. Recently emigrated, they had come from one of the stern little fishing ports on the northeast coast of England which is continuously under assault from the cold gray North Sea. One would have thought they would have welcomed the change, for Georgian Bay, with its rich red rocks and dark blue waters, at least looks a warmer and more congenial place. But when I asked how they liked it the wife said, "I dunno. It's all right. Kids like it. But I miss the salt. The air was salty at home. You could taste it." She looked out across the narrow harbor entrance to where a ribbon of bay could be seen shimmering in the afternoon sun, and sighed, "It's lovely, of course, but no salt. It doesn't seem like proper water, somehow."

I know how she felt, though not wholly agreeing with her; for to my mind any water that'll float a boat and lead it to somewhere new cannot fail to be proper water.

Georgian Bay is roughly rectangular in shape, lying northwest-southeast, with Port Severn in the southeastern corner and Killarney (whither I was bound) in the northwestern corner, a distance of about 120 miles, across a bay 60 miles wide. This was altogether too much open water for a 17-foot boat to take in one fell swoop. So I elected to drive up along the coast through the Thirty Thousand Islands to the Byng Inlet and make a 60-mile open-water crossing from there.

I haven't seen the Thousand Islands of the St. Lawrence, but I've glimpsed a few of the Ten Thousand Islands on the Gulf Coast of Florida, and I can't help feeling that it is pretty niggling to allow only 30,000 for all those islands on the east coast of Georgian Bay. Either that or careless counting. Or perhaps there is a size limit for islands, like fish, and you put the small ones back. So at what point does a rock become an island?

My Crusoe complex is very strongly developed. An island is an immediate challenge to me and I want to explore it on sight. I've lived on a few small islands and am not disillusioned. I look forward to living on several more. Even without the threat of that long crossing I would not have been able to resist a journey through the Thirty Thousand Islands. However, when I looked at the chart I was appalled.

In Norfolk, Virginia, I had been at the receiving end of one of those unlooked-for, unlikely, long-lost-uncle-remembers-you-in-his-will sort of gestures that happen every once in a while to perpetuate the belief in Santa Claus. The owner of a large ketch southward bound from the Great Lakes dumped into my lap a huge roll of charts saying: "You might as well have these. I'll never be going that way again."

Charts are a big item on a trip like mine and they are as indispensable for the safety and comfort of a voyage as the face mask is for a skin diver. The massive gift roll covered all the Great Lakes areas that I proposed to travel, and more, except for the Trent (the ketch being too big for this waterway), but I did not examine the Georgian Bay charts until I got to Peterborough. Then I cried in dismay, gift horse or not, "Oh, *no!* There must be something better than this!"

I was in the Outboard Marine offices at the time and it

was generally agreed that the charts were pretty horrible and that there would surely be better ones available. Not, however, in Peterborough, as it turned out.

No matter, there was a boat works at Honey Harbor in Georgian Bay, only twelve miles from Port Severn, that had everything, I was assured. If clear, legible, up-to-date charts were to be got anywhere, that's where they'd be.

My charts were not clear nor legible and certainly not up-to-date. They were made from surveys conducted in the nineties and preserved in the original manner of their printing. (I must make it clear that no reflection is intended on the generosity of the donor. The charts were the only kind available, as I found out.) They were printed without color differentiation between land and water, and where land and water intermingle to the extent they do in the Thirty Thousand Islands this can be very confusing. The print was very small, black on a white ground. Black dots depicted figures relating to the depth of water, rocks, channel markers, buoys, lights, islets and fly specks. Black lines outlined the shores and islands, so indented they looked like the outside edges of jigsaw pieces, and the overall effect was of someone having upset the black pepper on the tablecloth.

Large areas left white bore a legend reading succinctly "numerous rocks and islands." So numerous, in fact, that the surveyors had gotten fed up and gone home. Large areas left white without any legend indicated the surveyors hadn't gotten round to even thinking about them. The attitude conveyed by the charts was that those who knew the waters wouldn't need one and those who didn't shouldn't be there.

Ah well, I thought, I'll get this cleared up at Honey Harbor (a most appealing place-name).

There was of course the little matter of getting to Honey Harbor. And that, according to my chart, was impossible.

It allowed you to pick a way through a rock-field out of Port Severn until the rocks were so thick the printer's ink ran and there the channel gave up. Supposing one's boat at this point to be a helicopter, one could fly over that bit to clear water, land, and sail on in the ordinary way to the Honey Harbor approaches, where, according to the chart, the fun began again. More rocks, and only a hint here and there of a marker. Nothing convincing in the way of a channel at all. In fact the original cartographers thought so little of the necessity of strangers' being able to get to Honey Harbor that they printed the compass rose slap over the area, otherwise leaving it in pristine purity for the stranger to guess at the water's depth and what might lie submerged.

Yet from all I heard, Honey Harbor was a busy bustling place with boats going in and out all the time, and not all the boatmen using the harbor can have been born with a built-in fathometer and range-finder.

Perhaps I would be able to get a chart at Port Severn for Honey Harbor.

But I could not. I discussed the problem with local fishermen in Port Severn who looked at my chart uncomprehendingly and embarked on detailed directions along the lines of "turn left where the old red barn used to be and bear right at Tom's new pasture," interspersed with brief exchanges relating to complicated short cuts and finally condensing to a simple agreement that it would be all right if I went slowly and followed the bull's-eyes.

"Bull's-eyes?" I admit there is a lot I don't know about navigation.

"Yes," they affirmed, nodding vigorously, "on the rocks. Bull's-eyes." (I *had* heard right the first time.)

If I had been appalled by the sight of the chart, it was nothing to what I felt at the sight of the real thing.

It was a very lowering sky that frowned on my departure from Port Severn that morning. I tiptoed down the channel, out into the bay and to a vista that was hard to believe even looking directly at it. As if flung by giant handfuls, rocks lay scattered in the water with barely a boat's breadth between them, and were spread thus for miles. They were not rough and jagged as sea rocks are, but rounded and smooth, which by increasing the giant pebble illusion and giving a feeling of being lost on another world seemed to make them more menacing.

Good heavens, I thought, I'll never get through that lot. But by careful observation it was possible here and there to discern an occasional red or black stake, and sure enough, where it was not feasible to plant a stake, a bull's-eye was painted on a rock, with a black or red center to indicate on which side one was supposed to pass.

It took me two hours to get to Honey Harbor picking my way from marker to marker through the rocks.

Knowing what I know now, I guess I could make it in an hour and fifty-five minutes. I would not stop to gasp.

Honey Harbor is as delightful as its name. It is a village of islands. There must be some mainland about somewhere but I was not aware of it. Hotels, houses, churches and stores all seemed to have their own islands.

A low-lying outcrop of rock a few yards long with a stunted shrub in the middle of it bore a "For Sale" sign, and when I remarked on this at the village store, itself an island, there was a burst of laughter.

"The joke of it is," I was told, "the water's four feet lower than normal this summer. That's why the island is there. Usually most of it is under water."

"But surely it is not being offered for sale seriously?" I asked.

"Oh, yes. Islands are all the thing now. Everyone wants one. Some visitor will probably fall for it, and get a surprise when the water comes up again."

Honey Harbor is a summer resort, but the Despoilers haven't got there yet with their eternal gripes and insatiable demands, and it still has the atmosphere of a thriving country village. A Venice amongst villages, where the outboard takes the place of the bicycle and the jeep.

The water is full of little boats sizzling about importantly. Everyone drives an outboard, it is the only way of getting about; and it was pleasantly novel to see them being responsibly driven by schoolchildren, housewives out shopping with babies and baskets beside them, and little old ladies in prim churchgoing hats.

Most of the boats were open, skiff type, and built of wood. Fiberglas construction was rare. *Gemini* came in for quite a bit of attention. "Is that one of those plastic boats?" I was asked.

The Honey Harbor Boat Works, a very active concern, owned and operated by the Milner family, did not have anything new to offer in the way of charts, but did have a nice line in hospitality.

Despite the fact she had just undergone the treatment at Peterborough, *Gemini* was freshened up with a light overhaul and a new set of plugs, and given an overnight berth, all on the house. And I was asked to tea. A lovely tea-pot tea at Mrs. Milner's.

Tea is a very British institution, as I hardly need say, but it is one of the better minor ones. It takes care of the tag end of the afternoon when energies flag and it is too late to get started on anything else, and it recharges the batteries for the evening. If you have tea you don't gobble dinner as if you haven't seen food for a week and consequently you stay awake later. Also, it is useful for informal noncommittal social occasions.

The only snag about it, so far as I am concerned, is that I don't like tea. That is, unless I can make it myself, or get someone else to make it weak enough. Which is practically impossible, as there appears to be a social taboo on weak drinks, especially weak tea. People ask you how you like your tea and when you tell them they say, "Oh no, you can't possibly drink that," and hand you a cup of lye that removes the entire lining of your stomach in one swallow. Years ago in self-defense I learned to drown the tea in milk. Anyone can understand your wanting more milk, whereas they find incredible your wanting more hot water.

However, Mrs. Milner made splendid tea, and along with her daughters was eager to tell of the recent great occasion of the opening of the St. Lawrence Seaway and the Queen's visit. "You should have made your trip then," said Mrs. Milner, her eyes alight with the memory of an event already assuming legendary proportions. Everything that could float, she said, was taken out to greet the Queen, and I was shown photographs of the crush of boats round the Royal Yacht. It looked just like the Jersey Waterways on Sunday afternoon.

Charts are like kitchen space or cupboards. No matter how much or how many you have, you always want more.

Looking them over for the North Channel area, where I was soon to be cruising, I found more detailed ones were needed for the north side of Manitoulin Island. There were none available at the Boat Works, but Mr. Milner said they could be obtained at the Board of Trade Offices at Parry Sound, which was on my way. Then I found that in the journey from Honey Harbor to Parry Sound there was a twenty-mile gap in the black peppers for which no cartographic bridge was available. In view of the pilotage involved, I was rather dismayed. True, the charts were little better than moral support, but that is always better than nothing.

Mr. Milner was reassuring. "There's an inside channel," he said, "all the way to Parry Sound and it is so well marked you'll never need to look at a chart."

"They even use road signs," he added. "You can't possibly miss it."

It sounded like famous last words to me at the time but it was true enough. The road signs made their appearance near Parry Sound, and whilst a little startling at first, they seemed eminently sensible, especially in an area where innumerable streams all looking like the main channel lead off in every direction round innumerable islands and peninsulas. A curve sign on a point leaves no doubt as to which way the channel goes, and a SLOW sign by a narrows takes you through with a warning thrown in.

And despite the gap in the charts, there was no difficulty in getting to Parry Sound.

The boating boom had made such an impression on the Board of Trade (Canadian department of transport) that it had with commendable and unusual fervor and imagination set about improving conditions in order that boats would be encouraged to boom there in ever greater numbers and from ever farther afield.

The inside passage from Honey Harbor to Parry Sound was a result of these endeavors, a scenic and sheltered run in which one is never out of sight of a marker of some sort. Bull's-eyes, day-marks, lights, stakes are all there in profusion. It will be impossible to miss the channel when charts come out to match the buoys and one knows what they all mean. Such charts, I learned at the Board of Trade offices, were being made, but not knowing what they all meant certainly added zest to *my* pilotage.

The passage winds north through the Thirty Thousand Islands, islets, rocks, reefs and bars, with every so often channels branching off to small ports tucked away in the hinterland to the east. One would come round an island, islet, or some other thirty thousand obstruction and light on a single marker. It might be black or red, but only one, and just what did it mean? Was it part of the northbound channel, or one of those leading off into the interior? The answer was fairly important in waters which a survey-boat captain has described as being "sixty feet on the fathometer amidships and pounding on the bow."

Again, one might come on a pair of markers, a black and a red, but this did not necessarily denote a channel or that one should pass between them. They might be marking the outer edges of a shoal. . . .

These are the things that keep you young.

And, as I have said, there was really no difficulty in getting to Parry Sound. I took my cues from day-marks, which showed up clearly as white blobs in the distance. When in doubt over the position of a marker I looked round for an island with a white blob on it and took my direction from that, thus making fairly good time to Parry Sound.

There, at the Board of Trade wharves where I stopped to pick up the North Channel charts, I had an interesting conversation with the grizzled skipper of a survey-boat. He recited with exquisite detail every inch of the way of the passage from Parry Sound to Pointe au Baril. At Pointe au Baril I intended to "go to sea" and continue along the coast outside for fifteen miles or so to the Byng Inlet, where, if the weather was right, I would make my departure for Killarney on the other side of Georgian Bay. There was no point in following the coast round, because from the Byng Inlet onwards the shores were wild, shoal, and to all intents and purposes uncharted — practically, one might say, unchartable. An exciting coast to explore, but not one on which to be caught out.

I had hoped to make Pointe au Baril after leaving Parry Sound, charts in hand, landmarks in head, and eyes wide for day-marks; but a few blustery squalls with curtains of rain slowed me down and I stopped for the night in a cove appropriately named Snug Harbor. There the civilizing hand of man was only manifest in a dilapidated boathouse and a strong wooden jetty. It was quiet and still, an ideal spot to rest up and get ready for the crossing next day.

I ate supper, put things away in case the going was rough across the bay, and did a little work on course and distance calculations. I was about to turn in when there was a bumping alongside and a thunderous rapping on the cabin top.

I looked out, and in the dark made out three figures in a small fishing skiff. Two, muffled to the ears, crouched amidships. The other, standing authoritatively in the stern, was getting ready to deliver another fusillade which my appearance happily forestalled. He wore a black patch over one eye which gave him a piratical air.

"You can't come to Snug Harbor and just sit there," he announced. "You had better come back with us. It'll be much more fun."

"No doubt," said I, "but I'm off to Killarney tomorrow and want to make an early start. Thank you kindly, but I don't really want to go out tonight." (It sounded as though I was turning down an invitation to make a round of the local night spots.)

The Pirate wouldn't take no for an answer and called upon the other two to back him up.

"We won't keep you late," they promised. "We have to get up early, too. Come on." So I went.

We took off at high speed and went through a long cavernous creek where the rock walls rose sheer on either side and so closely as to muffle the motor. Finally we slid into a boathouse, left the boat there and climbed into a log cabin perched above, where oil lamps threw long shadows and a mellow golden light. Two college boys sat at a table demolishing a monumental feast.

"Now," said the Pirate, unwinding a long woolen scarf from around his neck, "we know who you are. But you don't know us. I am Alan Acres." He unwound the last of the scarf with a flourish and waved the end of it at the other two who had been in the boat and were now busily unmuffling themselves. "May I present Mr. and Mrs. Parr. They own that big fishing boat we passed on the way, only you couldn't see it on account of the dark. A pity, for it is a fine boat, and who knows when she'll sail again, commercial fishing being what it is. All the fish are gone from the lake and Mr. Parr is working for the Board of Trade. You must have passed some of his handiwork on the way to Parry Sound. Didn't you love the road signs? This is Roger, by the way" — one of the boys looked up from his diminishing plate and nodded—"and that's Gordon. They're on vacation. Roger does the cooking. To good effect, as one can see. Now, Miss Davison, what will you have to drink?"

"Well, I'll be darned," I said, "you do know who I am. But I don't see how. And no one knew I was coming here. I didn't myself, until I came."

"Smoke signals," said Alan. "You're out in the wilds now. Never underestimate the power of the bush telegraph. It knows what you are going to do sooner than you do yourself. Parr saw you at the Board of Trade today and recognized your boat when he came home tonight. You didn't say what you'd like to drink?"

From there the conversation naturally gravitated to smuggling, moonshine, shipwreck and murder.

"We're a lawless lot here, you know," said Alan with the satisfaction one can afford when the lawlessness is kept within certain gentlemanly bounds.

The evening passed quickly. When I got up to go Alan said, "You are writing a book, of course. Well, you've come to the right place, there's material here for a library, though you won't get any of it rushing through like this. However, if you must go in the morning you had better have breakfast with us first. I'll come by at half past six—early enough?—to pick you up and bring you here. You may not find this place otherwise, it is off the beaten track. Roger will cook breakfast and then we'll see you on your way. There are one or two places round here that are rather difficult when you don't know them, rocks you can't see and ranges hard to follow. Oh, and incidentally, don't get the bird sanctuary signs confused with the day-marks. Lots of people do and get into no end of trouble. The National Park people put them up to show which islands are strictly for the birds, if you'll excuse the expression. They're white boards like the day-marks, only a different shape. They all look alike in the distance."

"Oh." White blobs in the distance. "Would they be oblong sort of boards?" I asked.

Alan nodded.

Looking back over my trip along Georgian Bay through the Thirty Thousand Islands, I would say at a rough guess I must have navigated about sixty miles, all told, on bird sanctuary signs. At twenty miles an hour.

ii

WHEN I started out from Miami at the end of June Bert said he would take his summer holidays in September and meet me on the west coast of Florida ("You'll be there by then with that fast boat") so that we could put in some fly-fishing together on the rivers and lakes where the bass are supposed to be big and mean. As my progress did not live up to this optimistic estimation our meeting place moved farther north.

"We'll see New Orleans together."

Then, "Well, I guess it looks like St. Louis. . . ." But when I called from Honey Harbor on August 27th and Bert learned where I was he said, "Good God, is that all! I figured you'd be in Chicago by now, at least. What's the matter with this fast boat of yours?"

"Nothing, darling. These aren't particularly fast waters, and besides, I'm not trying to break records."

"That's for sure. At this rate, by the time I get to where *you* are, it'll be time to turn round and start back again. Where do you think you'll be by September 5th?"

The honest answer to that of course was "I don't know," but it wasn't a very satisfactory one.

"Do you think you can make Milwaukee by then?" Bert persisted, trying to pin me down.

"Six hundred miles in — lemmesee — nine days. On the face of it I could do so easily, but on past performance, improbably. I'll know better when I call you on Monday night."

And at that we had to leave it.

It was late in the year for the higher continental latitudes and the weather situation was becoming parlous. It could break any time and there was still a lot of Great Lakes sailing ahead — deep open water with plenty of punch in it — before I would reach sheltered waters again.

The good weather that had attended the journey along the Trent and through most of the Thirty Thousand Islands showed a little temper round Parry Sound, but had the good grace to see me across Georgian Bay.

Alan Acres called for me as promised and Roger cooked a monumental breakfast. After they had generously raided their stores to stock up mine ("Must have a well-found ship to take to sea") Alan and one of the boys drove along with me in their boat for a few miles to see that I didn't trip over any of their local propeller traps.

"I hope you have plenty of spare propellers," said Alan before we set out. "You are bound to hit something sooner or later, and these rocks are very hard. You don't have to be ashamed when you do, everybody does here even when they know the waters. Of course they maintain the rocks move. One old chap I know swears he's seen them do it."

So maybe the rocks down there liked me and moved out of my way. Anyway, I didn't hit a one of them.

The passage to Pointe au Baril was even lovelier than the preceding ones. The rocks seemed redder, the trees greener and the water bluer. The channel was even more involved, winding through the islands out into the bay and back again, and complicated by ranges placed at unexpected angles and so overgrown by trees that they were hard to see.

At Pointe au Baril I stopped for gas at the Ojibway Hotel, an enormous rambling wooden palace in the Victorian manner. It must have looked pretty startling when it was first built out there in the backwoods, with its towers and trimmings, but, over the years, it has mellowed surprisingly well. The Ojibway appeared to be populated, operated and overrun by boys and girls in their late teens and early twenties. Canada, they say, is a young country, and certainly at first glance it would appear to have more *young* people than any other kind.

They swarmed round *Gemini* in the weaving amorphic manner of the young.

"Wow!" they cried admiringly.

"Off to Killarney!" they cried enviously.

"It's a lovely day for it!" they cried wistfully.

And it was. Calm and sparkling, but with an opalescent visibility that reduced everything more than half a mile away to a translucent shadow. It was restful riding a compass course again, and it took only two hours to cross the benign, shining, but almost invisible bay.

Killarney had quite a different atmosphere from the

villages on the other side of Georgian Bay. It was as if I had crossed to a completely different country. Killarney looked like an outpost. It had a stark Hudson Bay quality about it, with the company store much in evidence, and the surroundings made the Thirty Thousand Islands cozy by comparison. Here the hills were high and precipitous, junior mountains with glistening white silica rock gleaming through the conifers like snow. It made one cold just to look at the view.

I refueled at Killarney, because in these parts it is wise to fill up the tanks when you can, and drove on to Little Current where I stopped for the night.

Little Current is the big city of Manitoulin Island, where a bridge spans the channel and connects the island to the mainland by road. It is a bleak-looking place in which the chief activity appears to be the unloading of coal. I woke up in the morning to find the entire boat, inside and out, covered with coal dust, the very air black with it and a thick coat lying on the water.

It began to drizzle, not enough to wash the coal dust away, just enough to make matters indescribably worse. As the docks lay downwind of the coal yards there was no point in attempting to clean up, so I cast off and drove down the coast to Gore Bay, a small village with extensive dockage in a deep inlet, 25 miles west.

A little further on the way, but not much.

I arrived there about noon and spent the rest of the day cleaning up. It was such an exasperating waste of good running time that next morning I didn't even look at the weather. I just set out.

I was now in the North Channel, cruising along the

north side of Manitoulin Island, and it was Monday, the day for my biweekly call to Bert, the last before he started out from Miami on his way north. It was important to aim for a harbor on the telephone system, by no means a *sine qua non* for harbors in the area; and according to the Pilot Book, Meldrum Bay, at the western end of Manitoulin Island, appeared to be the safest bet.

Manitoulin is almost 100 miles long — the largest fresh-water island in the world — and, with the smaller islands, Cockburn (Canada) and Drummond (U.S.A.), divides the North Channel from Lake Huron. It is wild and spectacular, heavily wooded, with bold high bluffs and deeply indented bays and inlets. All of which was so much hearsay so far as I was concerned on the morning I left Gore Bay, since land and water were both shrouded in thick rolling mists. There was also a stiff wind blowing; northern climes have the dubious ability to create fog and wind at the same time.

The waves became very aggressive, and it was plain that if I had any sense I would go back to Gore Bay and use the telephone there. But go *back?* When it was so vital to go *on?* Meldrum Bay was only thirty miles away and it was thirty miles *on* the way, so I went on, bumpily and not very fast, but *on*. None of this back stuff.

In half an hour a line squall had blown the world apart, whipped it white and passed to leave a half gale and a violent head sea.

Still I wasn't about to turn back. But it had become apparent that even if *I* was going on, *Gemini* wasn't. She was going up and down in the same place like a rocking horse and with much the same short motion. Temporarily calling it quits, I crept into the tenuous lee offered by Cape Robert, the western arm enclosing Barrie Sound, and anchored there, close to the point to save time in the event of a quick change in the weather. Such *wishful* thinking.

In no time, of course, the wind veered and Cape Robert was rendered useless as protection. The wind blew straight past the cape down into the sound, sweeping the seas before it, piling them up into big rolling graybeards and blowing spray off the crests in long horizontal streams.

It was impossible to stay where I was or go anywhere but with the wind, so I upped anchor and wallowed down into Barrie Sound to look for shelter. I found it in a shallow stony cove in the lee of a tightly wooded but uninhabited island in—according to my chart—uncharted waters.

At seven o'clock that evening I was sitting in the cabin listening to banshees howling, haunted by a picture of Bert waiting for the phone I knew darned well wasn't going to ring.

The banshees howled all night and up to half past nine next morning, when I thought they didn't sound quite so frantic and ventured out for another try at Meldrum Bay. This time I made it, and the first thing I did there was to call Bert at his office.

The village telephone was in the general store behind the post-office section of the counter, open to the eyes and ears of the world. It was a hand-cranked steam-age model and making a connection to tropical Florida was quite a feat. A lengthy feat, during which everyone in the store tiptoed about ostentatiously *not* listening.

Finally Bert was on the line, his voice distorted by static and reduced to a midget travesty, but dear and welcome. There are times when "hullo" is the most beautiful word in the English language.

In stentorian bellows I told him what had happened and gathered that he responded with something like "I thought so," which was rather disappointing. Then he said he was leaving in the morning for Indianapolis to spend a couple of days with his brother and departing again on Saturday for Milwaukee. Did I think I would be there by then?

The gist of my reply was that if the weather didn't improve, *no*. When and where should I call him next for further conference?

Friday night, he said, at his brother's, and gave me the phone number. I wrote it down on a piece of paper, thoughtfully put in front of me with a pencil at that moment, and wound up the conversation to everyone's satisfaction by yelling "*And I love you too,*" after which business in the store was resumed as usual.

The weather did not improve. It got worse, and if Meldrum Bay hadn't been such a delightful place I would have been spitting with frustration like a jungle cat. But the picturesque old fishing village, which looked as if it had been transported en bloc from Nova Scotia or Newfoundland or some other outpost on the North Atlantic, kept me fairly quiet with modified outpost amusements such as wild mink and tame deer.

Fishing on commerical lines had long been abandoned

in the village and fishing boats and fish house rotted on the beach in artistic decay. But fishing kept the village going all the same, for the whole district is an angler's paradise. Devotees unable to get out on the water fished from the docks to the joy and edification of a wild mink, who lived in the jungle of pilings and stole the catches as fast as they were made.

The deer was at a pheasant farm at the far end of the village. A retired couple ran the farm. They had no help, and it was a rubber-boot, unremitting operation. But it was a lifelong dream come true and they were content. They took me round the farm and I was shown pheasants in every stage of development from egg to adult, thousands of them, pecking their lives away. The deer came out of the woods when called, a slender, elegant creature who gently accepted our offerings, thus bartering his only defense — wariness — for the dubious friendship of mankind.

In spite of local diversions, waiting for weather was an unsettling business, and I waited and waited. But the weather relentlessly continued to be boisterous and wet.

A cruiser on a tight holiday schedule came in and went out again. Enviously I watched her go, big enough to plow into the stuff.

The interisland steamer came in and went out. I watched her go, and waited.

The days crawled by, windier and wetter by the minute.

I wrote and sketched and cleaned the boat, hung the curtains about five times a day, stared at the sky, prowled the dock, sat up, stood down, and invariably ended up by going to the store for something I didn't need in order to lessen my gloom by spreading it.

Ivan Trick owned the store and minded it. Through the shop windows he kept an eye on the bay so that he could be on the docks to meet boats coming in; for he was also harbormaster, dockmaster, customs officer and steamer agent. Outside the store were two fuel pumps belonging to Trick. They took care of the needs of passing motorists and transient boatmen. The Meldrum Bay postmaster and the Meldrum Bay telegraph operator both were Ivan Trick, of course. A busy man, but you'd never know it. He raised neither dust nor voice. But he was a ready listener as he went about his business, weighing this or stamping that and keeping a watch on the bay. And he had a conjuror's genius for finding items you wanted that he did not have in stock.

Thursday came, the day before I was due to call Bert and break the news of my whereabouts. Suddenly in the late afternoon, too late, the dirty black clouds rolled up into clean white bundles against a bright blue cloth and the heavenly laundry was done.

The sun shone, low and golden, and Meldrum Bay was transformed. Hitherto it had worn a mournful aspect, but now there was a riotous rich patchwork of blues, greens, reds, browns and purples, deep satisfying colors, broadly treated. It is incredible how hungry one gets for color after a steady diet of grays. I could never bear northern winters again. Far too pallid — my eyes would starve. They feasted now, and my morale went up like a rocket. But it didn't last. During the night the familiar drumming on the cabin top began again with a fresh downpour of rain and the familiar wind song wailed in the trees. On Friday morning Meldrum Bay was gray again and the North Channel was churning up in its usual miserable manner.

I did think, though, that some of the fury had gone out of it, that it might possibly be fit to travel tomorrow. But oh dear, what to tell Bert?

At the appointed time I went to the store, opened my purse to get out the slip of paper with the Indianapolis number, and couldn't find it.

I turned the contents of my purse out and searched them piecemeal. Not there. I searched my pockets. Not there. I went back to the boat and searched, even to the garbage bag. The paper with the phone number had inexplicably vanished.

I knew the address, so back I went to the store and called Information, who denied the existence of any such address or any such people. An unlisted number. Unassailable and unobtainable.

It was evening and there were a lot of people in the store, as much to pass the time as for shopping. Faced with the promise of an interesting drama, they draped themselves on boxes and chairs or leaned on the counter and made no bones about listening.

I said: "Oh, well, if I can't call him, I'll wire this phone number and he can call me."

But Ivan Trick in his quiet voice said, "It won't go out until nine o'clock tomorrow morning."

Nine o'clock tomorrow morning Bert would be well on his way to Milwaukee.

I explained this and people coming into the store were shushed. It surely was a dilemma. Everyone could see that. We had Bert arriving in Milwaukee and disconsolately searching the waterfront, not knowing where to look next or how to find me. And I wouldn't know where he was or how to get in touch with him. It really seemed we two might never meet again, until Ivan Trick suggested calling the police.

"The *police?* How do they come into this?"

"You call the Indianapolis police and explain the situation to them, give them your husband's address there and this telephone number, then they'll get in touch with him, give him this number and he can call you."

"Do you think they'll do that?" I said doubtfully.

"Why not? You can at least try."

Feeling, as I so often do in my life, that events were getting away from me, I asked the operator for an Indianapolis police station. Which one? Oh . . . er . . . the main one, I guess. Huh. Now the operators were in on it and the problem was getting international coverage.

Of course it was hours past the time I had arranged to call Bert and once again I had visions of him waiting.

After being passed along the line from operator to operator I found myself diffidently unfolding my tale — with some assistance from the prompter's corner — to the Indianapolis police. To me the story seemed more implausible by the minute, and it became harder and harder to sound convincing. Then suddenly I realized I had a sympathetic ear. Nay, *more*, the guardian of law and order, bless him, understood the situation exactly and was willing and eager to re-establish communications in the Billheimer family. "We'll get in touch with your husband right away," he promised. "Now your number is . . ."

And it wasn't so long after that Bert was saying in his diminished telephone voice, "Hey — I thought they'd caught you smuggling when that police car arrived."

"They sent a *police car*," I relayed to the fascinated audience to Bert's bewilderment. "Who dat?" "People." "*What* people?" "Interested people." "Oh," said Bert, "I bet. Do you think you can get out of there tomorrow?"

We beat round the possibilities of meeting places, some of them suggested by the interested people, and finally decided on Detour, a fifty-mile run for me and a lot farther, though more certain, one for Bert. He reckoned on making it by late afternoon, and I — who knows? We arranged to keep contact through Ivan Trick, if the weather did not permit and I was unable to leave or got caught out somewhere.

A gusty sigh passed round the store when at last I hung up, mission accomplished. It was half past ten. Ivan started putting up the shutters. The show was over.

Strangely enough the weather did permit, and the Billheimers were reunited at Detour without further mischance. But not for long, as it turned out.

iii

"BUS to Detour?" said the man behind the counter. "Hell, no, nothing goes down that road but rabbits and Indians."

"Well, how about one between here and Manistique?" asked Bert.

"Here" was St. Ignace, where we were following up a Bright Idea in the bus station. It was the day after we had met in Detour (so aptly named) and a stinker, a half gale from Alaska, wet, windy and cold. Seasonable, as the locals pointed out, and only to be expected.

There were forty miles of Lake Huron and four hundred miles of Lake Michigan to be traversed before Chicago and sheltered waters again. At this time of year it meant that anything even resembling a traveling day would have to be used as such. If one waited too long there was a good chance of being frozen in for the winter. However, Bert and I had no intention of spending his holidays playing tag on land and lake with hardly ever the twain meeting, so we brought our brains to bear and worked out a relay system whereby we could be together and travel, too.

We would leave the car, drive the boat to the next

port of call, return to the car by bus and drive it back to the boat. Involved but companionable.

Since Chicago was at the southern end of Lake Michigan (favoring the west side), one could get there by following either east or west shores. I elected to take the west shore route, which meant a run along the top of the lake, where harbors are scarce. There were only two suitable for a day's run from Detour: St. Ignace, forty miles from Detour, and Manistique, eighty miles from St. Ignace.

This being definitely a non-boating day, we had decided to make a dry run over the course and case the ports for fuel pumps and dockage and look into the bus situation.

At the bus station in St. Ignace we learned there were no buses to Detour, but that there were to and from Manistique. Very well, then, we would travel separately to St. Ignace and start our relay race from there.

St. Ignace or, as the locals say, St. Igness was primarily a ferry port, connecting points in the state of Michigan separated by the Straits of Mackinac. Its importance has been lessened somewhat since the completion of a bridge across the Straits, but ferries still ply on a vast schedule and have unassailable holiday appeal. And of course there is no other way for the tourist to reach Mackinac Island, a popular resort six or seven miles offshore on the Huron side of the straits.

There were several small boat docks in the wide horseshoe harbor of St. Ignace and for our meeting we chose one which had a parking lot overlooking the water (so reminiscent: No dear, not under the clock. Let's meet somewhere that I can sit down, in case you're late).

I hoped I would be able to recognize the place from seaward.

The drive from St. Ignace to Manistique made it abundantly clear that it would be a one-shot trip. There was nowhere along the shoal and barren coast where one could put in for fuel and shelter. The gray lake flashed white with breaking waves and looked most uninviting.

"It'll have to do better than this tomorrow," we said.

And the next day dawned with a beetling sky reflecting darkly in waters of oiled silk. A sinister dawn crammed with threats and portents. But calm.

St. Ignace was only forty miles away. "A two-hour run," I said, incurably optimistic. "Should be there before anything blows up."

"Well," said Bert, "if you are not there in four hours, I'll drive back along the shore looking for you."

The day before we had noted emergency landing grounds along this bit of the run from the road.

The calm didn't last long; it never does when you are counting on it. A huge swell rolled in from the east followed by a wind from the west, and the weather settled down to a real good go of the miseries, just as it had promised. At Mackinac Island *Gemini*, gamely doing her rocking horse act, could barely make headway. There was no sign of a letup and at the rate of progress I was making it would have taken the rest of the day to get to St. Ignace. Heaven knew where Bert would be by then.

Oh no, I thought, we're not going through that again. This wind won't stop the ferries.

So I altered course to the island harbor, left the boat there and leapt aboard a ferry which was quivering with the imminence of departure.

As it cast off I realized there was a fare to be paid — only a few cents — but all the money I had was a fifty-dollar traveler's check, a form of currency which often panics outback traders convinced that all checks are illegal tender. I was bound and determined to go to St. Ignace. Change was found.

Winning an argument or a game is quite often only a matter of psychological determination.

As the ferry entered the harbor I looked for the dock at which we were to meet, but the small-boat docks were at the other end of the town and I was not sure I could see it. Certainly I could not see any sign of our little yellow car. A wild hope occurred that Bert might have thought of what I was doing and was meeting the island ferries on the off chance I'd be on one. I scanned the line of cars waiting at the ferry docks. No yellow ones. No sign of Bert in the waiting throng.

As soon as the ship berthed I rushed ashore and hurled myself into the nearest cab.

"Where to, lady?"

I stared at the dirver. I didn't know.

"Take me to . . . I want to go to a small-boat dock at the other end of town. There's a red pump on the dock. . . . No, a yellow one. . . ."

It was the driver's turn to stare. He turned round and did so pretty steadily.

I was uncomfortably aware that I looked as wild as I sounded.

"I'll know it when I see it," I amended lamely. "There's a large parking lot close by. It's way off, down at the other end of town. Please hurry."

"It'll be Red's place," decided the driver, slipping into gear. "They all go there."

But it wasn't Red's place. I knew that at once.

"This is where the yacht-boats come to," insisted the driver. "Ain't you meeting someone?"

"Yes, but not in . . . what's that place over there? See, with a red pump on the dock? Take me there."

But that wasn't it, either.

"There *must* be other small-boat docks." But I had to tell the driver the whole story before I could allay his alarm and engage his cooperation. We then started on a systematic search of the boat docks in St. Ignace.

There was a chance that Bert was looking for me at any one of them on the premise that I might not have recognized our rendezvous from the water.

The four hours were up, of course, but it seemed likely that under the prevailing conditions he would allow a little more time before driving back along the coast. However, there was no sign of him or the car anywhere.

We had exhausted the small-boat docks, and were just about to start on another circuit of them, when a little yellow English Ford darted out of a side street, nipped ahead and disappeared round a corner on the road leading out of town to Detour.

"That's it!" I cried. "There he goes! Quick — follow that car!" And thought, How like the movies life does get sometimes.

It was fully five minutes later, the old cab swinging on the corners, tires squealing, horn screaming, the driver marveling, "For Pete's sake, what's he got under that hood?" before the cacophony astern impinged itself on Bert's consciousness and the Billheimers were united yet once more.

"Well," said Bert as we ambled less strenuously back to St. Ignace, "where do we spend the night — with the boat or the car?"

"Boat," I said. "Let's see Mackinac Island whilst we are about it."

We parked the car, hopped on a ferry and tracked over the saltless sea, somewhat less rambunctious now, to Mackinac Island. We selected a hotel near the boat.

It was an enormous old-fashioned hotel, towered and gabled, with high ceilings, fancy plasterwork, sagging floors, illimitable ramifications, and apparently run by children.

The foyer was full of them. Small packs in conclave over the differing aspects of hotel management. We registered at the desk, presided over by a small girl of eleven, and were taken to our room by a young man of seven.

Invisible children filled the corridors with sound. There were intermittent slammings of doors, reverberations of drumming feet (whoever said they patter?), muffled scuffles, giggles, small shrieks and sudden pregnant silences.

During our short stay we saw no other visitors or adults in the hotel. There was probably some mundane explanation for this unusual situation. It was the end of the season and the entire island was closing down for the winter. One could assume that there were no reservations for that night nor any expected, and that the management had felt safe in taking the day off, dismissing the staff and leaving the kids in charge. But how dull to assume such things! We declined to probe. It wouldn't have been wise anyway, because judging by the peculiar behavior of the objects in our room, there is a possibility that the hotel was run by leprechauns.

It was a very large room and overlooked the harbor through high bay windows. A pleasant room but . . . Windows jammed open or shut, depending on which they were and what you wanted. Drapes flew wider when the cords to close them were pulled. Light bulbs, hanging naked on three fathoms of cord, blew at the touch of a switch, and blinds, untouched by hand, fell without warning and with hair-raising crashes. A strategically placed but neatly disguised tear in the carpet never failed to trip one on the way to the bathroom where the hot water tap in the basin ran cold, and the cold water tap in the shower sent out a cloud of steam.

Bert said, "These holidays are *rough*," and flung himself on the bed. I took a shower, and after I'd been alternately frozen and scalded, discovered there were no towels. Nobody answered either bell or phone and finally Bert was induced to rise from his recuperating couch and go on safari in search of towels, whilst I nipped in and out of the shower for quick scalds to keep warm.

"Only one?" I cried, on his return, grabbing it.

"That's all they could find," said he.

The hotel dining room was closed, we learned with relief — God knows what the kitchen might have come up with — and although this meant we had to go out, hunger now superseded fatigue.

A heated discussion was going on behind the desk as we passed. An older girl, fourteen at least, was upbraiding the child clerk who had signed us in. "Whaddaya mean renting that room for only nine bucks? Ya dope. Ya couldda got . . ." But what she couldda got we'll never know, for they saw us then, and the discussion broke down in deep, far-reaching blushes.

There was a false bustle in the streets as crowds disembarked from the ferries to take a last look round before the shutters went up for the winter. Shops did a lighthearted business, with packing cases and paper strewn on the floors. The air was charged with liberation, an end-of-term, school's-out feeling. Only the horses looked as though they felt business was as usual. No cars are allowed on the island. There are bicycles for hire and ride- or drive-yourself horses, and chauffeur-driven surreys for the non-experimentally inclined. A bicycle for two, or a horse each, would have been irresistible if it had not been so late or our hunger so great, but our desires were centered on food and we were having a hard time finding it.

Most of the restaurants were already closed, and we were neither dressed for, nor in the mood for, a grand-style dinner at a grand-style hotel. Several shop windows bore notices reading DO NOT EAT IN THE STORE, which was puzzling until we found one with the postscript LICKING FINGERS IS NOT ENOUGH.

We finally ended up licking our fingers at an Olde Hotte Dogge (this pernicious idiocy has spread to the States, I am sorry to say) Stand, which of course was out of dogs.

We woke to a quiescent dawn showing portents for neither good nor ill, and loped over to St. Ignace to refuel ourselves and the boat. We called the weather bureau there (who referred us back to the Coast Guard station at Mackinac Island) and discovered that a south-west wind of 25-30 m.p.h. was the order of the day. If true, this would make it an extremely eviscerating, if not impossible, trip. But sometimes one has hunches about these things. We both had a hunch that the weatherman was out of line, and feeling strongly thus, we set out.

A white fog was billowing about in the straits when we went through; it blotted out the sight of the new bridge, which we saw as one massive piling disappearing heavenward like Jack's beanstalk. And despite some opposition from a pale autumnal sun, fog came and went for most of the trip, coming, of course, whenever we wanted to check our course on a buoy, light or land-mark. Consequently, we flew blind to Seul Choix Pointe, a cape not very far from our destination — and glad we were to see it, though neither of us would admit it.

Manistique we achieved in four hours and twenty minutes with some assistance from an unscheduled east wind, so we gave our hunches a pat on the back.

The yacht club at Manistique has comfortable sheltered dockage with nice low quays for small boats, and the club members hovering about welcomed us warmly. Leisurely we settled the boat, securing bumpers and tidying up the inevitable journey clutter, making fast and desultory conversation all the while.

Casually I inquired when the bus went to St. Ignace.

"Well, now," said a club member looking at his watch, "it ought to be along any minute."

"Where do we catch it?" we gasped, springing ashore.

"About four blocks . . . turn right . . . by the drug store . . ." came floating after us as we pelted down the road.

The bus rolled up as we reached the stop and we swung aboard to ride eighty miles back to St. Ignace. There we unparked the car and drove eighty miles back to Manistique. "Getting to know you," sang Bert as we rolled along the increasingly familiar shoreline.

"This," he said later, as we stumbled into our motel beds, "is the most frantic holiday I've ever had. Is it *always* like this with you?"

iv

NOTHING had prepared me for the desolate wastes of the north Middle West. Michigan for me had connoted Detroit, and all the appurtenances of big business and industry, hustle, bustle, glitter and grillwork. No matter that Detroit was not actually on Lake Michigan, it was in the state of the same name, and the one, so far as I was concerned, stood for all. I have quite a genius for collecting geographical misconceptions, which is one of the reasons I find travel so fascinating — I am always being surprised. And the wastes of Michigan astonished me.

It was all right for Canada to have some wilderness. In fact it would have been disappointing if there hadn't been any. My associations for Canada conjured trappers, snowshoes, "mush," Hudson Bay and that sort of thing. Outposts on Georgian Bay and in the North Channel were satisfyingly "in character," but frontiers on Lake Michigan — ! It was like meeting a woman *en déshabillé* and discovering she was both younger and prettier than you thought.

I had looked in vain (and with growing delight) for the jazzy marinas, the white-winged yachts, the fancy cruisers and the yachting-capped lads speaking the argot of the pseudo-psalt, which had made up my mental picture of the boating-yachting activities on Lake Michigan. Instead, I found lonely waters and windswept shores, curlew-haunted sand dunes and long curves of lonely white beaches backed by vast stands of silent forest. It was harder to refuel in Lake Michigan than in Georgian Bay and much harder to find shelter. There are very few natural harbors on the north and western shores of the lake (indeed, in the north, very few harbors at all); north and west, the harbors are man-made, protected by sea walls. The bold barren coastline is intimidating, but fascinating, too, in a bleak sort of way. It has a negative attraction, and pleases more for what it has not than for what it has. As there is no civilization to speak of, there are none of the shabbier aspects, no tinsel, no gauds, no garbage.

The scene gradually changes as one travels farther south. The wilderness becomes less stern, until finally it gives way to the placid dairylands of Wisconsin. There, neat, orderly farms punctuate the low, level cliffs with barns and silos and cattle dotting smooth pastures. Small towns begin to appear with their harbors before them, enclosed in sea walls like the fenced-in gardens of English homes. Farther south still, the scene grows more industrial. Larger towns appear, with, of course, larger front gardens.

At first though, way up at the top of the lake, there were only those wastes, miles of lonely shores, where Manistique was the only harbor, and the only boat I saw was a small fishing boat, its crew crouched behind a canvas shelter, heading for home like a scalded cat.

By the time we reached Manistique, Bert had only two days left of his holiday, and we spent them trying to keep warm. The temperature plummeted, the wind howled and the rain came down in torrents. We ventured out in the car once, during a brief lull, to see if we could find a stream wherein to cast a fly (neither of us moves a foot without a fly rod in the luggage) but the lull was short-lived and we soon gave up that idea. We returned to our motel to read drug store mysteries and cook a compensating steak on *Gemini's* picnic stove.

The third, departure morning dawned wan but clear, and we set out on our separate, solitary ways back to Miami.

I had no definite destination in mind for that day; the aim was to get as far as possible. I wanted to get home now, and was all set to pile up the miles. Now at last it could be truly said I was on my *way* home, for at Manistique, for the first time, my journey turned south and henceforth, until it ended at Miami, would be towards the sun.

Husband, home and sun. I drove out of Manistique Harbor filled with determination to mop up the lake in a couple of days, and in twenty minutes was back in port with the motors sniveling, for a change of plugs.

Plugs changed, and with ardor undiminished, I drove out again, determined to mop up the lake in two and a half days. After some brisk running for an hour or so, I put into Washington Island on the edge of Green Bay to top up the tanks. A rather secretive channel wound its way into Jackson Harbor, which, for all its name suggests, turned out to be a ramshackle but pleasing fishing village nestling in reeds and willows by a mirror-like pool. Rough timber jetties staggered out uncertainly into the water, but there was nothing resembling a fuel pump. The fishing boats at Jackson Harbor, I learned, were refueled from drums brought from the mainland. Since mine was only a precautionary measure, I decided to carry on farther south. Bailey's Harbor, I was told, had all sorts of fueling facilities.

It went against the grain to leave unexplored such a promising island, with its wooded hills, bluffs and gorges, but for once the urge to get on overcame my curiosity.

Up to then it had been a pleasant ride on lazy water with the sky in that condition described by amateur photographers' aids as "cloudy bright." The weather gave a classic example of the bright period between horrors that occurs in northern climes just often enough to persuade people to endure what are otherwise intolerable conditions. But as a rule, bright interludes do not last long, and this was no exception. Shortly after I left Washington Island, small cat's-paw squalls dabbed the water, rippling and dimpling it; then with dramatic suddenness, a snorting southeaster was blowing and whipping the ripples and dimples into full-grown waves with whitecaps. The wind was coming from an awkward quarter for my course, so I wasn't sorry when Bailey's Harbor came into view. Not that it appeared to offer very much, a broad horseshoe bay about three miles deep and two across. It was wide open to the southerlies and so far as one could see from outside there was no harbor.

However, the fuel situation now was such that I could not afford to go looking for another place on this lonely coast with the wind the way it was and getting worse by the minute. I turned into the bay thinking that you often have to get very close to shelter before you see it.

Tucked away in the northwest corner of the bay, a red and white village peeped through the trees, but there was nothing in the way of a landing there. The erstwhile sea wall was in ruins, mounds of concrete and rubble, useless except for agile anglers. It served as a rough windbreak, however, and I considered anchoring in the lee of it and wading ashore to find a garage and refuel with the aid of cans. Not a very appealing notion and fortunately canceled by the announcement from a fisherman scrambling over the wreck of the sea wall that there were docks across the bay.

Through binoculars, I checked this assertion, but could not see anything other than cliffs, woods and stony promontories. But the fisherman held to his course. "That's where the boats go when they come in here," he insisted. Well, I thought, where the boats go, there go I. And off I went across the bay, where sure enough there were docks: a combined Coast Guard station and commercial fishing base whose earthwork jetties blended nicely with the background and were adequately protected by shoals and fingers of land in a way not apparent from afar.

Two fishing boats moored there charmed me by their resolute functionalism. They were absolutely basic boats, making not a single pretense to comfort, beauty or anything other than their sole purpose of being waterborne fish carriers. One was made of wood and the other of steel. Battered, unpainted, singularly unlovely, they were named, tersely, aptly and respectively *Tub* and *Can*.

There were no fuel pumps. It appeared that as a general rule, the passing boatman passed. But the genial fish company boss made a space for *Gemini* alongside one of the earthwork jetties and organized a fueling party which involved several willing hands, a truck, a drum on the back of the truck, a hose pipe, a filter, much backing and filling, heave-ho-ing and luck. It was not exactly what I had understood by the rumors at Washington Island that there were "all kinds of fueling facilities at Bailey's Harbor," but it was certainly *one* kind. And it worked, providentially, without the loss of a drop or a temper.

Bailey's Harbor is on the Lake Michigan side of a long island or peninsula, a finger of Wisconsin, that encloses the lower half of Green Bay on its eastern side. The harbor — "where the boats go" — is completely separate from the village, and they are even farther apart by land than by water. The road between them winds grass-centered and apologetic through forest, and the measure of the solitude is plain in the number of deer one sees browsing by the roadside.

A more direct contrast to Milwaukee, where I landed a couple of days later, could hardly be imagined. Another of travel's little attractions — the contrasts, it's all or nothing, rags to riches, and not too much of either, which is oh, so much better than the dead level of mediocrity.

There was an intermediate stop at a strange little

place lying between the arms of two rivers and called, in the succinct manner of these parts, "Two Rivers," where *Gemini* lay by a scaffold and bobbed ceaselessly in the wake of passing outboards. The two rivers are navigable upstream for about two miles only; when the lake is rough, as it was then, the outboard faction of the town is compelled to drive up and down the rivers to let off steam, which they did with unabated speed and enthusiasm for hours on end.

Next morning *Gemini* made the best run of the trip up to that point, eighty-two miles to Milwaukee in three hours and thirty-five minutes.

At Milwaukee I was back in a familiar America where building-block towers make jagged geometric skylines and the atmosphere is electric with expectancy, efficiency, enterprise and bustle.

Milwaukee stands on the lake behind long and massive sea walls (a very large garden this, almost a park), a busy little port and a progressive industrial town. Handsome, I thought, and jolly, though this it could hardly fail to be, seeing that its two main products are beer and outboard motors.

The beer is of several kinds, but the outboards are Evinrudes, and as my Heavenly Twins were of the same breed, it was old home week for them; and I had a wonderful time in Milwaukee. The outstanding activity, of course, was a visit to the plant where the motors are assembled. There I made a round of inspection (like royalty) on an impudent little two-seater scooter truck (not perhaps so much like royalty after all) and had a new model — as it was then — trotted out for me in its bath, all seventy-five rampaging stallions snorting and pawing in their impatience to get away and really show their paces.

Motors of all sizes, in every stage of development, from the embryo to the complete assemblage, hung in chains from overhead railways, along which they were moved to each stage of construction. Rows and rows of bright new hoods (bonnets in England — better to have bees in) waited in colorful array to be matched to their appropriate engines.

Since my knowledge of engines was on the "go" or "no go" lines there wasn't much I could offer in the way of convincing comment. I would have liked to, too — everyone was so enthusiastic and the machinery was so active, "ooh" and "ah" didn't seem nearly enough. I wondered how royalty came by those pat little phrases they seem to be able to satisfy everyone with on *their* tours of inspection. But perhaps they don't have any — perhaps being royal is enough. They can say "the cook has boiled the baby again," and with the right expression everyone would be delighted. But I don't believe that would work for me, somehow.

Variety, they say, is the spice of life. Those people are always saying things, and in this instance they could as well say "contrast." But you can oversalt the stew, too. After Milwaukee, a coal dump. And all because of the fear of losing face.

Whenever you arrive anywhere by boat the first question you are asked is "When are you leaving?" It is a bit daunting at first, but you get used to it, so when this question was shot at me in my first five minutes in Milwaukee I said nonchalantly, "Thursday morning" (the first day that came into my head). Everyone was being so very organized that I thought I had better be specific. Whereupon arrangements were set up for a Thursday morning departure.

When Thursday arrived black-visaged with spindrift flying on the lake, I wished I hadn't been quite so definite, and if someone had said, "Surely you are not going out in this?" I would have allowed myself to be persuaded to stay a little longer. But nobody said anything but "How long do you think it will take you to get to Chicago?" so I figured this was the sort of weather outboard boaters took in their stride in these parts, and of course I could do no less. I tried to look intrepid and devil-may-care, and pressed on nervously with departure preparations.

To my surprise, because nothing of the sort had been mooted, two outboard boats drove out of the harbor with me, one on either side, and proceeded to escort me down the lake.

We belted along side by side, leaping from crag to crag, grinning and waving and jolting coccyx up to cranium with the shock of our landings in the troughs, but none of us moved the throttles back one fraction of an inch. No sir. We were upholding our various honors even if it broke our backs. Fortunately, before that happened the escort signaled they were going home and turned back. Though I envied them I bravely carried on until they were small in the distance, then I stopped, seized the chart and looked for the nearest harbor south.

This proved to be only five miles further on, but when I got there it was to find the docks of the yacht club in the harbor absolutely untenable from the implacable surge that swept in from the lake through the harbor entrance. I turned to the river — all lake towns seem to be on rivers — and followed it upstream in search of a mooring. The river banks were revetted but for the most part highly fenced, which made it difficult to get ashore, and of course the few good places were already taken. The dank and dingy day did nothing for the town, which gave a feeling of having given up hope long ago; dispiritedly, I taxied up and down the river until finally I spied a small space between two hulks by a coal dump, and edged in. An old man with a four-day beard appeared like a genie out of the ground to take my lines, which he made fast, moving in an unexpectedly smart, seamanlike manner.

"You'll be all right here," he said, and was rather touchingly grateful for the small reward I gave him. "A libation," he said, "thank you, ma'am." He straightened and nodded, a twinkle in his faded eyes, and stumped off with an anticipatory spring in his mariner's stride.

I could have done with a libation myself, and wished I had been one of those impervious Victorian females who used to charge across continents with a lorgnette, an umbrella and enough assurance to intimidate a Turk; then I would have gone with the old man, and after we had toasted the downfall of our enemies I might have found out what an obviously expatriate sailor was doing so far from the sea.

As it was, I went ashore for stores and was timidly approached by a shy pale youth who muttered something inaudibly at me. I thought he was asking for the time or directions and stopped. He mumbled again staring at his feet, and after a while I discovered he was trying to suggest we had met before. I said no, I was a stranger in town and didn't even know where there was a telephone, which was what I was looking for. He said there was one a few blocks down the road and shyly walked there with me. Then we solemnly shook hands and he wandered aimlessly away as I called Bert.

Back at the boat I watched large fat rats exploring the interstices of the revetments. They would stop on a beam level with the cockpit coaming and wave their whisker antennae inquiringly in my direction.

Next morning I was in Chicago, name-dropping like mad to obtain a berth in an exclusive and crowded yacht basin.

Chicago charmed me by its bright vigor. I had not expected to like the place, but I did. The skyline is superb. The massive buildings have a scrubbed look about them. The streets are wide and the whole atmosphere is one of tremendous vitality. A city of superlatives, in which everything is bigger, brighter, better and faster than anywhere else. Especially faster. Never have I seen such traffic. Crossing the road on foot was a terrifying experience. Cars swooped and swirled at jet-like speeds, in and out and around one another, glinting and winking on overpasses, underpasses, thru-ways and expressways, a spectrum of movement, a fast-flowing, endless stream.

It lived up to its reputation as the Windy City all the time I was there, miniature gales bowling down the streets, creating whirlwinds at every corner to catch hats and skirts and take your breath away. And it *almost* lived up to another reputation for which it is more widely, though less happily, known.

The incident occurred shortly after I had arrived. Chicago was a mail port for me and the collection of mail for a boatman is one of the most urgent needs after disembarking — not counting a shower! The post office incorporating the general delivery department was a long distance from the yacht club and I was glad of the offer a club member made to drive me there.

On the way he failed to make a fast enough getaway at a change of light to please the truck driver astern, who put his hand on the horn and held it there as a measure of his displeasure.

We were in a street constricted by the massive supports of an overhead railway, so the truck could not pass us easily, and my driver saw to it that he could not pass at all. Moreover he slowed down to ten miles an hour. A very rude gesture this, in Chicago.

"That'll fix the sonofabitch," said my driver.

Frenzied hoots and shouts followed our funereal progress.

At the next light, which turned red before we got there, my driver pulled over a little, whereon the truck whirled past, pulled over diagonally across our bows, and stopped. The driver swung out of his cab, and strolled over to us, shoulders hunched, arms hanging and fingers curled in the manner familiar to devotees of the television screen.

Well, well, I thought, Chicago welcomes you.

Putting a great paw on the car top, the truck driver leaned over and snarled through the window.

"What's wid you, wise guy?" he said.

I could hardly believe my ears. They really do say this?

"Wanna make something of it?" replied my driver, sticking strictly to the script.

They were both big men and they bristled at one another ferociously. I settled down in my front-row seat to watch the play unfold. The dialogue was hackneyed, but I thought the action might be different. They were evenly matched. How far would they get before the cops came, I wondered. Supposing the truck driver had a knife? He looked ugly enough for anything. Perhaps they would shoot it out.

But the action in the play was no better than the dialogue, after all. The light turned green and the traffic behind us shrieked on their horns with impatience. The truck driver scrambled back to his truck, cursing.

And that was all. . . .

PART FOUR

Rivers

i

AT REGULAR intervals, which seemed to come closer together all the time, I had a deadline to meet for magazine articles, which meant I had to find somewhere to stop and write. One of these occasions came up whilst I was in Chicago, but Chicago was no place for writing, at least for me. For all its size and luxury, the yacht basin there has very little in the way of shelter, and a constant surge off the lake kept *Gemini* in a constant state of agitation, creating a condition *not* conducive to writing aboard. On the other hand, I didn't want to go ashore and write, as that meant too much of an upheaval. All the bits and pieces to be taken ashore—typewriter, paper, carbon, notes and references—and inevitably something of vital import would be forgotten and I would waste time building up a solid mental block trying to avoid going and getting it and yet be quite unable to work without it. Then there's the business of getting used to one's surroundings before being able to work in them.

Surroundings are very important, I find. If they are beautiful I have to have my stare-ful first, and if they are ugly I cannot stand them and have to move. Sometimes they are just plain irritating, though not apparently so at first, and it is imperative that I circle round in them at the beginning, like a dog on its bed, before I can relax and take them for granted and get down to work.

Sometimes the circling takes quite a while. It is tiresome being so temperamental, but there it is, and I have given up fighting it now, just as I've got used to the idea I am five-four and a half and will *never* be tall.

Gemini's cabin was small, but it was familiar and everything was quite literally at hand, so all that really remained to set up the required working conditions was a quiet mooring for my "studio."

This should not be too difficult I thought, for the next part of the journey was over a thousand miles down river to New Orleans, and surely somewhere along the way there would be an inspiring anchorage? Not perhaps on the first few miles out of Chicago on the Drainage Canal (now called the Sanitary Canal — no improvement, to my mind) but surely on the Illinois or Mississippi rivers?

And the way time was going the sooner I found one the better.

It was a blustery wet morning when I set out to look for a quiet mooring and I bounced across the windy outer harbor to the lock, gateway to the — ugh — canal. The lock-tender there said, "I knew someone was coming across because of the spray, but I couldn't see your boat at all." This gateway lock at Chicago was vastly different from the other locks I had been through. It was big enough to hold a regatta in, and there was so little difference in the water levels that I didn't even have time to catch hold of anything before I was waved on through.

The canal goes right through the heart of town. The huge buildings are so close to the water that the solid stone revetments seem to rise up to meet them, and with the numerous bridges overhead, one after the other in quick succession, the general impression is that one is driving through the very buildings themselves.

It was slow going through Chicago, but I expected to make up for lost time as soon as I got outside. One thing I thought, the weather can't hold me up much now. But the weather can affect adversely by remote control, it seems, for no sooner had I cleared the environs of Chicago than I came up behind a towboat and could not get past. The barges were in ballast, and the strong cross-wind kept blowing them clear across the canal.

I had now embarked on inland waters where the commercial traffic was heavy and profuse. Coveys of barges strung out in line several abreast, up to as many as forty-eight in a single tow, travel the watery highways of the Middle West's great rivers, conveying vast quantities of freight for hundreds — even thousands — of miles. A single barge may be as long as 300 feet, and a tow well over a thousand. Although always referred to as tows, most of them are in fact *pushed* by the enormously powerful towboats peculiar to the rivers. A wise small-boat skipper treats the tows with awe and respect and gives them all rights of way under any circumstances everywhere. It takes a tow several miles to stop, they leave a wake of very heavy weather the effect of which is felt up to five miles away, and the barges create a suction there'd be no withstanding if one inadvertently got too close. So one doesn't just toot and pass a tow, especially in constricted waters. One first sees that the way is clear well ahead, and then overtakes with infinite caution, keeping as far from the tow as possible without getting too close to the bank, for the wash there can put a small boat ashore (this once happened to me in a sailboat — most embarrassing). Moreover, the backwash off the revetment wants watching too.

The tow I got behind on the Drainage Canal was comparatively small, and for once it was really being towed, but the tugboat was underpowered for the job and had very little control over its light and flighty charges. Every time the way was clear ahead the wind caught the barges and swept them majestically across the canal whilst the tugboat huffed and puffed in vain. When disaster seemed inevitable it made a last desperate effort and somehow regained temporary control. Then for a few minutes the tow would travel straight and level, so to speak. But then of course there would be a bend in the canal or a tow would be coming the other way. So I was compelled to stay behind at five miles an hour — all the way to the depot, for those in the house who can remember trams — wondering, I must admit with a certain fascination, whether the tow was going to make it or pile up. And whether it did in fact reach its destination or simply gave up, I don't know, but finally it pulled into a lay-by, to my relief and no doubt to the tugboat skipper's too.

The bridges on the Illinois River, it was interesting

to note, all bore evidence on their gouged and scarred pilings of the difficulties of towboat navigation.

Once off the Drainage Canal and rid of the recalcitrant tow, the traveling was fine and fast, but only in spurts, for then there were locks to contend with. Big wide locks to accommodate the gigantic tows, and deep, with drops of over forty feet to carry those tows over otherwise impassable falls and rapids. When the wind blew in the bottom of these locks it was as much as I could do to hold the boat. She plunged and strained like a frightened horse, and I was glad she wasn't a thirty-footer. But despite the vastness of the operation and the intensely commercial aspect of it, the lock-keepers on these locks were just as friendly and helpful as those on the smaller systems I had been through. One even replaced my windshield wiper blade which had flipped overboard from a too-vigorous wipe just before entering the lock. A windshield wiper is as essential on a boat of *Gemini*'s type as it is on a car, and I grizzled about losing it to the lock-tender simply to let off steam, because I certainly didn't expect to be able to do anything about it there.

However, he said, "Just a minute. I think we've got one of those here," and disappeared into the power plant.

It seemed an odd thing to happen to have handy in a lock, but sure enough, that was just what they had. When I tried to pay for it my offer was waved away impatiently. "It's just an old blade. It'll do until you can get a new one."

In point of fact it worked so well I never did have to replace it.

The Illinois is a broad and stately river winding through splendid rolling country which is interspersed here and there with great heaps of gorgeous craggy bluffs. The river towns have musical flowing names like Peoria or Meredosia, or exotic ones like Pekin, Havana or Peru. Since the Illinois is a powerful river and prone to flooding, many of the towns are walled like mediaeval cities. One, Beardstown, has a wall that rises sheer from the water fifty or sixty feet, so high that from the river the town is invisible. I had intended to stop there for the night, but for the life of me could not see the way in through the wall. As it was almost dark I hurried on downstream to where there was a small floating dock by a bridge, and in order to tie up, I had to tilt the motors to step over submarine cables.

The Illinois was an inspiring river all right, but all the same it wasn't easy to find somewhere to write. Partly because I was somewhat in the frame of mind of a motorist who, with a long way to go, passes up restaurant after restaurant — "wrong side of the road . . . don't like the look of it . . . passed that one anyway" — and partly because I belong to that school of writers who seem unable to perform except under extreme pressure — that is, the deadline has to be so imminent it would seem to be impossible to meet it.

This particular moment of truth arrived — after I had turned down several fairly likely spots for fairly invalid reasons — just above the point where the Illinois joins the Mississippi River, and influenced by the time factor, I thought I had found the ideal place. A tiny basin entered by a boat-wide creek, shaded, and it seemed quiet. But alas for the muse, it turned out to be a jolly center for bonhommous boatmen imbued with a determination to unconfine joy. I fled. But the river was shrouded in fog, and I bethought me of the tows and returned ignominiously to the basin to champ amid gaiety until the fog lifted. As soon as it did I shot out again without paying any attention to what the weather was up to. It happened to be blowing rather hard and from ahead, but I bounced along, single-minded in my search for a suitable writing anchorage.

After a very short time I was just as single-minded in a search for any old shelter, for the wind increased considerably.

It is very wide — a mile or so — at the confluence of the two rivers, and since the reach there is about twenty miles long, a wind has quite a distance to work up a punch in the water. When it happens to be working against a strong current as it was in this case, the result is apt to be discouraging to boatmen. Several boats out for a Saturday afternoon's basking quickly scattered for shelter and I looked round pretty sharply for some myself.

There was none to be had immediately on the Illinois side of the river. There, the shores rise abruptly in precipitous palisades, though one boat crawled optimistically under an overhanging tree and made fast to the branches. But according to the chart, more conservative protection was likely to be found further downstream at Portage des Sioux, on the opposite, Missouri, side of the river (which, incidentally, by then has become the Mississippi only). It was a six-mile run and took nearly an hour against the harsh steep seas of the river. But it was all rather providential, as it turned out; the harbor I chose quite haphazardly at Portage des Sioux, a small village of many harbors, proved to be exactly what I was looking for, providing not only perfect shelter for the boat but ideal conditions for the writer.

In real life, however, perfection is a seldom thing. There's always a fly in the ointment, they say (there They are again, and what sort of ointment do They use, I wonder, I've never yet found a fly in any) and the fly in the ointment of my harbor (how far-fetched can one get in this metaphor business?) was tornado threats.

During the ten days I spent in Venetian Harbor at Portage there were tornado warnings in force nearly every day. Actually, like the Chicago truck driver's ire, they came to nothing, but one never knew. There were short sporadic gales, torrential downfalls of tropical intensity, and long-drawn-out thunderstorms in which incessant lightning bathed the darkened countryside in a weird flickering purple light. And a funnel was sighted only six miles away.

The great winds of northern gales or tropical hurricanes cause widespread and terrible devastation, but there are certain steps one can take to avoid absolute dissolution. A tornado is intense, selective, personal in its destruction, its path is narrow but unpredictable, and where it strikes annihilation is complete and unavoidable. It is like a bomb in that there is no defense against a direct hit. For sheer horror there is nothing to equal the bewildering results of a tornado. A man comes home in good faith and finds his house and family gone. Completely erased, vanished truly and tragically into thin air, with nothing anywhere, ever, to show they had existed. And the houses on either side untouched.

It is well known that inhabitants of earthquake and volcanic districts come to regard their malignant phenomena with indifference. The Portage villagers, living in a tornado area, were casual too. When I spoke to them about the possibility of one striking, they shrugged and said, "We have a cellar," as one might say, "We have a talisman," and they'd add, "You can hear them coming — they roar like an express train."

I wrote my story with one ear alert for the approach of an express train.

Occasionally between warnings there would be some good hours when the skies were bright and then I would stiffly put aside the typewriter and wander down to the village to see it and find out how the outside world was getting on.

It was a real country village, in spite of its fancy name. I walked there from the harbor through stubble fields and long winding country lanes and the silence was marvelous. I seldom heard a plane and there were few cars. There were only country sounds, isolated but clear in themselves, without the perpetual hum of traffic through which most of us spend our lives hearing things.

The one village store I could find — it was a curiously sprawling village without anything pertaining to a main street — had the usual fascinating heterogeneous conglomeration of goods which seemed to meet most of today's rather exacting requirements, including such important frivolities as home permanents. The post office was cleverly disguised in a wing of a neat white house in which lived the postmistress. I went searching for it in order to mail some books home, and when I found it at last, I nearly got into deep trouble.

Bert and I are both omnivorous, insatiable readers, though I do not believe he quite shares my fidelity to individual books. I cannot and will not do without books; they are my instructors, friends and confidants, to whom I refer over and over again, and woe betide anyone who borrows one of my books and fails to return it; he's made an implacable enemy for life. My peregrinations are always accompanied by an increasing load of books, which has been much lightened of late by the growing ubiquity and scope of paperbacks, a blessing I perceived to be somewhat mixed when I tried to send some home through the Portage mails.

The books were tied up in bundles without any paper wrapping, so that the whole world could see they were just a bunch of old paperback whodunits, but the postmistress reared away from them as if they'd bite and said, "I'm afraid I cannot accept those."

I thought she meant they were not wrapped or tied properly, but then I saw the whole place was plastered with posters of the "Help Stamp Out Pornography" persuasion and light dawned.

I'd grown so used to the lurid covers of paperback mysteries I was no longer aware of them. The busty blonde in disarray never bore any relation to the contents of the book anyway, and I had come to accept her as part of the makeup, like the size of the book or the quality of its paper. Not so the postmistress. To her the hussies on my bundles of books proclaimed pornography loud and clear and she wasn't about to let them contaminate *her* mail.

Poor Perry Mason! Who'd have thought it! And really Portage wasn't that far off the map — how was it possible that anyone there could never have seen such books before?

It was quite some time before the postmistress was convinced that the books were innocent, legal and obtainable by anyone at any drugstore, dime store, newsstand or supermarket and that they were non-corrupting and fit to be sent through the U. S. Post Office mails.

During the process of conversion — or at any rate the attainment of acquiescence — I had a chance to take a fresh look at the cover girls in question, and I must say they're a fairly salacious-looking lot, though anyone who could be corrupted by them would have to be pretty weak in the head. I felt perfectly safe in sending them home to my husband, when at last they were permitted to go, and I returned to my story-making on *Gemini* wondering what the good lady's reaction would be to a perusal of some of the present-day best-sellers.

The Venetian Harbor at Portage fulfilled my writing requirements perfectly. It was extraordinarily quiet and peaceful in itself (it could hardly be blamed for the tornado warnings and the general *Sturm und Drang* of the weather) and the setting was lovely. The covered slips, decoratively shaded by tall trees at the back of them, were arranged round a harbor pool so still and landlocked it might have been a small lake, and although the country round about was flat, by the harbor it sloped towards the river in gentle dips and hollows.

It was an old-fashioned harbor in one respect, in that it was a family concern. A close-knit and charming group who knew how to be helpful without being overbearing, a quality that is more rare than one would think.

The slips were all in very good condition and supplied with electrical outlets and water taps, which is nothing unusual in yacht basins of this type. But what was new to me was the actual *modus operandi,* which I had not come across in boating before (though I understand it is practiced fairly commonly on the rivers). The slips are not rented in the ordinary way, but sold, and the buyer then pays a monthly maintenance fee. Although there is a small gas dock, transient boatmen are not catered to at all. Of course, I had no idea of the situation the day I arrived, all windswept and aggravated, looking for shelter and a hideout. But it so happened that there was a vacant slip which the harbor management generously allowed me to use without any charge.

The most popular type of boat in the harbor, and indeed generally on the river, was the houseboat, and they were treated by their owners as country cottages, somewhere to get away from it all. So every weekend, rain or shine, the houseboats were occupied. If the weather was good they might go out and take a turn round the river to get in some fishing or swimming or just a little plain boating, but it wasn't essential to move. If the weather was bad or a person didn't feel very energetic, it was mighty pleasant right there in the harbor, far better than stewing away in St. Louis or Granite City.

I went for a ride in one of these country cottages and was very impressed. It was a fast cottage, commodious, and handled very well. Time was when I would have snorted at the very idea of a houseboat as a *boat*—it was a contradiction in terms, if not directly agin nature. But I must say it was very soothing sitting out there on the back porch, gin-and-tonic in hand, watching the world go by at a smart clip, and before we got back my admiration was growing slightly green round the edges with envy. I began to dream about a houseboat on the West Coast of Florida.

However, dreams were quickly carried away on the tides of reality. Here it was October and high time I was on my way.

By the sixth I had finished my story and mailed it. As there was no fog and it was not actually blowing a gale, there was no reason for delaying my departure, but I set out uneasily nonetheless. The river had been rough before, but now there was something more. It was rising and gathering speed, and as it rose it gathered debris from off the banks and bars and from around the little island shores and swirled it along, swiftly, silently, menacingly and inexorably.

All over the country little rivers and streams were swelling from the recent and continuing heavy rains, and feeding bigger rivers, which were growing even bigger. The Mississippi was in flood.

Under wet gray skies I threaded my way downriver from Portage through logs and branches and an occasional tree — all making very good time, I noted — and at Alton Lock I met a red nun buoy behaving in an alarming manner. Its moorings were shortened by the rising water level, and it plunged and strained, swinging from side to side as if it was alive and in an agony to get free. Later, in St. Louis, I was to see a nun that had broken away. It was rocking down the Mississippi at nine knots, sweeping through the town, past the bridges, dipping, nodding, curtsying, spinning, weaving a mad dance to freedom and the sea.

I went through Alton Lock alone except for a log jam, and at St. Louis noticed how the water bulged against the massive bridge supports. I stopped for fuel at the Mound City Yacht Basin and as I turned upstream to come alongside the gas dock I found it was necessary to gun the boat to the point of plane to prevent it from being swept away by the current. I decided to stop over and review the situation.

I wanted to see St. Louis anyway. The Blues had long been one of my favorite tunes. I might as well see the evening sun go down there as anywhere.

ii

LOCAL knowledge is one of the hardest things to come by. It is difficult enough to get simple directions on the road but, as I have noted before, it is even worse on the water. Maps, charts, pilot books tell most of the story, but local knowledge would help so much. Mostly it doesn't, though, and the reason seems to be the apparently inevitable desire of human beings to be popular by pleasing.

Anthropologists are always quick to defend the quirks of the tribes they are anthropologizing in faraway places. "They are not liars, these people," we are earnestly informed, "they want to be accommodating by telling *you* what they think *you* want to know."

But why do they have to go to the utmost ends of the earth to find out such things when the natives much nearer home have the same quaint little ways?

My problem was really quite simple. All I wanted to know was, was this the river's normal condition, or did it ever slow down and become clear of debris? Should I press on regardless, as it used to be said, or would it pay me to wait?

I hadn't liked the way the river was behaving on the run down from Portage, and the next morning at St.

Louis I liked the look of it even less. It was still rising, crawling up the river gauge hand-over-hand and disquietingly gathering more speed along with bigger and better bundles of debris. Great rafts of logs and whole islands of trees with part of the embankment still clinging to the roots whirled by, and small-boat navigation grew less appealing by the minute.

Yet, if conditions can get worse, it is not unreasonable to assume they can also get better. But how long would it take for the river to improve — days, weeks, months? *Years?* And how good was better?

But the Old China Hands considered me rather than my queries. If they thought I was a death-or-glory gal they said: "What's a little ol' river to you after that great big ocean, heh-heh? Just keep upwind of the debris and you'll be all right. The current'll give you an extra tèn knots — and with your boat you'll be in New Orleans in a week."

But if they happened to be of the school that look upon women as Members of the Weaker Sex, they would make long faces and tell me in mournful numbers: "The river's tough. Those sinkholes can swallow up a boat like yours. Gas is hard to get, you'll have to have a range of at least two hundred miles. Then there's the blue logs — those logs that've been about the river so long they've sunk and lain on the bottom for years, till gases in the wood float them up again. Only they float just under the surface and you can't see them, but hit one and it'll rip the bottom out of your boat. See that guy over there? He lost his boat on a blue log last week."

"And how about the tows, huh? Your motor cuts out

in front of one of those and *gerzunk!* The skipper doesn't see you and he couldn't stop if he did. The suction draws you in and down you go like a stone."

"You think this is debris? This ain't *nothing*. You should see the river in a real flood. Then the stuff's so thick you can walk on it clear across to the other side. I remember . . ."

Bad news, I reflected, not only travels fast, it talks more; and it doesn't answer questions either, it just discourages. Rather despairingly, I *almost* considered the possibilities of trailing the boat to New Orleans or shipping it down on a barge. But fortunately before such heresies took any real shape in my mind I thought of all the unlikely craft and people that have made the trip down the Mississippi, and figured if they could, I could. I decided to stay awhile in St. Louis and find out how to navigate the river without getting mixed up with the trees. If nothing else, I would be getting used to the idea. Trouble has a way of diminishing after being squarely looked in the eye for long enough. Sometimes.

St. Louis is an exciting town, though a passer-by could hardly be aware of this, for it has a drab, uninspiring exterior. Even the waterfront, where one normally looks for the picturesque, is a dispirited conglomeration of cobblestones, railways, billboards and tired old red-brick, half-empty buildings. And the river, for all its romantic associations, contributes nothing in the way of charm and beauty. It hurries through the town, a vast swirling outpouring of liquid mud. The fastest mud in the West.

Some of the old showboats, the stern-wheelers inseparable from river lore, still linger on at the foot of the steep cobbled levees to earn, after a lifetime of glamour, what seems to be a slightly seedy retirement as bars, clubs and theaters. A melodrama is played nightly aboard one of the superannuated showboats and the proper atmosphere is created by the audience cheering the hero and hissing the villain to their just deserts.

Modern showboats carry out the tradition of high-jinks on the water, but bear little resemblance to their forebears. The largest and most modern excursion boat looks like a water-borne dirigible. It is streamlined and silver, built of steel and carries 4000 passengers on five decks. There is a ballroom aboard to accommodate a thousand couples and the other two thousand people can disport themselves in the amusement arcades or otherwise about the various decks whilst waiting to dance. The vessel is a marvel of construction, but too new yet to be picturesque, whereas the old showboats at the foot of the levee have gone beyond it. Had I stayed, as originally intended, only long enough to see but one evening sun go down, I most probably would have gone on my way under the impression that St. Louis was a pretty dull town.

What the casual passer-by misses, of course, is the fascinating double life in St. Louis: the steelworker who is a poet, the engineer who is an artist, the insurance agent who builds little sailboats, the storekeeper who writes books. Maybe the Mississippi mud is fertile soil for the muses — they seem to flourish along its banks — or maybe, so far as St. Louis is concerned, it is the jazz in the background music that stirs them up or spurs them on there. Whatever the reason there does seem to be a higher proportion of one-off character jobs and fewer run-of-the-mill status-seekers in St. Louis than in most other similar-sized towns.

It is not unusual, of course, for people to have a bent outside their living, but in most communities these days, self-expression is suspect and any talent not developed professionally is best practiced in secret if social acceptance is valued. In St. Louis the arts are allowed to overflow into everyday life unremarked, much as they do in Ireland, where everyone is an artist of some sort and the smallest bistro is likely to double as an art gallery or theater.

One is more apt to discover this aspect of St. Louis by boat, for the river has a tight hold on the imagination of the townspeople. Everyone yearns to make a trip on it, again if they have done so already, and one and all keep a sharp eye on waterfront activities. No boatman could hope to slip through St. Louis unnoticed. The Mississippi has undoubtedly one of the hottest grapevines extant and a new boat in town is at once in the spotlight of attention. All sorts of people trooped down the swinging docks — a chain of steel barges linked together like sausages which had a most disconcerting habit of punctuating every footstep with a resounding *Boing* — to bow themselves on and off *Gemini.*

Among the first was a young Englishman then at the University of Illinois. He arrived quite unheralded one evening with a borrowed car ("I hope this is the right key. Can't think what all these knobs and things are for, can you?") and a somewhat uncharacteristic invitation to go out and see the town. He suggested the Crystal Palace.

"A local jazz joint," he explained, "rather amusing if you haven't seen it. If you like jazz?"

I like jazz.

The Crystal Palace was noncommittal on the outside and dark as a tomb inside, though I got an impression of a lot of red plush, stained glass and mahogany, Victoriana which may have suggested itself in the flickering aurora cast by the candle-lit glass chandeliers and candelabra that hung about and gave the place its name.

An upright piano, a double bass and a microphone stood on a small dais that served for a stage, around which wooden chairs were packed in tight formation. We groped about and found a couple of empty seats, but it wasn't easy. I can never understand why it is considered essential in the States to eat, drink and be merry in public in an almost total absence of light. On the assumption that women look better in a subdued light, can it be that Americans believe they look best when they cannot be seen at all?

Waiters fought through the press of people for orders and we justified our presence with beer as a defense against forfeits, for the entertainment was not confined to jazz. The lively young man mastering the ceremonies conjured members of the audience onto the stage from time to time to render a piece of home-grown verse or prose, and in one case, a demonstration of "three-dimensional music." This was done by a large man in a conventional blue suit, sporting a bushy beard to show he wasn't as conventional as all that, who stepped onto the platform with a small kerosene cooking stove. He got the stove going with only the normal amount of fuss and smoke, and then, with some fancy flourishes, broke half a dozen eggs into a saucepan. To the accompaniment of a jungle beat on the double bass the eggs were stirred over the fire, slowly at first, then faster as the beat increased in tempo, until a frenzied climax was reached and the pan was swung aloft and tipped, to decant the now scrambled eggs onto the front rows of the audience below.

All this time, and in fact throughout the evening, an impervious artist worked on a backdrop at the back of the stage. He painted without any apparent reference to a prior design, and worked from a stepladder, climbing up and down it and moving it about, in front of and around piano and performers no matter what was taking place on the stage. Brushwork that struck the audience as specially choice was enthusiastically applauded (often to the complete bafflement of the performer then holding forth) and once the M.C. dragged the artist off his work to be presented to the audience, at whom he glared with fury until the introduction was over and he was released. Whereupon he darted back to his element, a fish off the hook.

I must say his theme was developing in a most interesting manner, but we did not stay long enough to find out what it was all about.

A couple came to *Gemini* one morning with a businesslike air, saying they'd read about her and would like to look her over, as they believed she might be the type of boat they were looking for, for their cruising. After scanning her narrowly and nodding cryptically, they offered to drive me downtown, which was fine, because I was about to go shopping for stores and welcomed a ride. So we drove off in their truck and they dropped me off at the Markets.

Now these markets were not, I discovered, the dazzling American supermarkets which stupefy us outlanders by the fantastic volume and variety of goods they stock; they were the old-fashioned markets where several storekeepers vie with one another under one roof. Ah, but with what wares they vied! Real old-fashioned food with *flavor!* And texture. And all sorts of delectable qualities that have been lost in modern processing.

Although it may not seem like it sometimes, I am really crazy on progress. I am mad about laundromats and all the things that smooth the path, I am entranced by space science and wonder drugs, but I do wish they'd leave some of the wildernesses alone and the taste in food. There is a whole generation now that does not know how bread, butter, cheese, beer and honestly aged meat used to taste. And they probably wouldn't like it if they did, poor saps; food is so mixed up with those tiresome early emotions that we all grow up with a predilection for the pies that mother used to make. But the fact of the matter is that mother has been making some pretty pallid pies of late. Of course they're very pretty, those pies, but what happened to the flavor? This modern business of eye-appeal in the food department is being overdone, and it doesn't fool my taste buds one bit.

Happily those who like *living,* like to eat, and as long

as there are a few individualistic strongholds such as St. Louis around there'll be a few oases in the culinary desert where rich ripe flavors will obtain.

St. Louis is also a carnival town. Its answer to New Orleans's Mardi Gras is the Parade of the Veiled Prophet, which happened to take place whilst I was staying in St. Louis. I was dragged off the boat to see it, as unwilling as the artist was to be dragged off his painting in the Crystal Palace, and feeling about carnivals as he did about meeting the public. However, for those who like carnivals, St. Louis has one. As entertainment I personally, if regrettably, preferred the fight that cleared a restaurant where I had dinner a few nights later.

"I thought you might like dinner here," said Rusty. "It is supposed to have a very English atmosphere."

The attractive young redhead with shoulder-length hair had materialized on the dock by *Gemini* earlier in the evening in the pouring rain. Oh God, I thought, the woman's angle again. But it turned out that Rusty was a flying instructor as well as radio and meteorological officer for an aircraft construction firm, a woman of wide interests and a diplomat to boot.

"I've read some of your books," she said, "and when I heard you were here . . . I just had to come down. . . . I wanted to ask you some questions about England. I am, that is a friend and I are, planning a boat trip over there. Perhaps if you're free, you'd have dinner with me and we could talk?"

Of course we could. So, the restaurant we went to was decorous in dark oak, with here and there bottle glass, hunting scenes, toby jugs and pewter mugs to give the proper English accent. It was also a little brighter than usual. We sat in a booth by the wall. Next to us several tables had been pushed together to make one long one for a party of about a dozen. It was quite a quiet party, gay enough, but in a *sotto voce* manner as became the surroundings.

"What sort of a boat trip do you plan in England?" I asked after we'd studied the menu, placed our orders and settled down to boil plots. Then I listened appalled, finding myself cast in the unenviable role of an Oh-but-you-can't-do-thatter. (How many times has it been said to me? And how much energy have I expended — wasted? — in proving I could, too, do just that.)

"But Rusty," I said plunging in, "England hasn't got inland waterways like the States. A boat suitable for cruising round the coast wouldn't be any good for the canals and rivers, even if you could get it from one to the other."

"Oh." Rusty looked so downcast I felt responsible and tried to make amends. "Of course I've been away for a long time," I began — shades of the obliging natives, not that long! — and finished lamely, "but I guess the English Channel and the Irish Sea are much the same as they were." And the North Sea. And the River Thames and Lake Windermere and all those skinny little canals. No, I must stick to my guns.

"If you want to see England from a *small* boat like *Gemini*, why don't you put it on a trailer." A trailer? On those rolling, winding English roads? And how about launching? I didn't even know if there were any launching ramps in England now, or what, if any, facilities there were for trailer-boating. Last time I was there, boating was mostly sailing, and seagoing stuff at that, and outboards were ferocious little pop-bottles about as reliable as the weather and waspish in sound and temper.

"Couldn't I sail round the coast?"

"*All* round the coast — the whole of the British Isles?"

Rusty nodded.

"Oh dear, that's a big undertaking." The bigness of it so engrossed us that when the first table went over it did not impress us as anything more than a dropped tray. However, two trays are not as a rule dropped in quick succession, and the second crash brought us smartly back from England just in time to see the third table go over.

The decorum of the party next to us had come undone.

Crockery, glass, knives and forks flew in all directions as a gasping, grunting melee of men surged back and forth, bulldozing tables and chairs in their path.

We stared in petrified amazement. It was as implausible as the hostess whipping out a switch-blade and going berserk at a soiree.

The disintegration of the party was complete. The girls had gone, banished like conjurer's rabbits. Only the men remained, furious, struggling and curiously silent. Equally silent, dumbstruck, other diners stared, dinner forgotten, until someone screamed. Then, like a flock of startled birds, they rose and scattered for the doors. One woman mistakenly ran to a kitchen door and beat on it shrieking at the top of her voice, but the kitchen staff within had apparently barricaded against the enemy.

The scene changed swiftly, as in a film, and the restaurant was empty, except for the combatants and Rusty and I. It never occurred to us to move.

Rusty leaned across the table and said: "Oh, Ann, I'm so sorry. It isn't usually like this here, I assure you."

Then suddenly, the storm was over. The struggling bunch resolved itself into two panting groups, each holding a man, bloodied and torn—the nuclei of the disturbance. The two men were still beside themselves with rage and the issue, whatever it was, was still apparently unsettled. One of these men was a minor colossus, bull-necked and bloodshot, and I was horrified at my immediate, unreasoning reaction of revulsion and fury at him, picking him as the villain of a situation about which I knew nothing at all.

Waiters began to appear, nervously, one by one, as if out of cracks and crevices to which they were ready to return at the first sign of recurring violence. Policemen strode in through the street doors accompanied by a man looking harassed enough to be the manager. Oblivious of their approach, Bull-neck tried to open another attack, but to the delight of the tiger I keep caged within me and who leaps exulting to the bars at the first sign of strife, he was outnumbered, and the whole mess of angry men was swept outside.

Waiters, clucking, began to pick up the pieces.

"Well," said Rusty to one, "do you think you can take care of our order now?"

"For heaven's sake," he replied, "have you been there all the time?"

"Yes, indeed," said Rusty. "And where were you? I

didn't see you about, doing anything towards breaking it up?"

"No, ma'am," said the waiter with a grin. "You sure didn't. I stayed right there in that kitchen behind locked doors. Didn't you notice — one of those guys was a very big man?"

We dined in an empty restaurant that night, but never got round to solving Rusty's sailing problems. The air was too charged with violence, and we could not stop speculating as to what all the bother had been about. Every now and then Rusty would apologize, refusing to believe my assertion it was the most unusual floor show I'd seen in years.

Day after day went by and the river continued to rise. Bigger and better debris hurled by, spreading farther and farther across the river. Cars drowned on the levee and the docks were wound in closer and closer to the shore. The difference between flood and drought, the highest and lowest levels of the river, is about 60 feet. A flash flood raises the level 20 feet or so with no trouble at all. But there is nothing predictable about these changes as there is with tides. Constant vigilance is called for but not always given, and people are always getting caught out. The long steep levees are used extensively as parking lots when the river is low, but it is surprising how many people forget that it doesn't stay that way forever. The result is good business for the garage people and motor salesmen. I saw several cars being towed up out of the river and Captain Bill, owner of the yacht docks where I rode out my indecision in St. Louis, grinned and said, "They will do it every time."

River docks have to float. Sometimes old boats are used for the purpose, but more often they are made from strings of old barges, steel or wood, which are attached to the shore by cables and winched in and out as the water rises and falls. A narrow, wobbly gangplank bridges the gap between ship and shore. Bill said it was not unheard of to have the whole works — docks, boats, cables and all — carry away on a big flood. He was much amused at the way I was fascinated by the debris. I'd never seen anything like it. The stuff in New York Harbor was peanuts in comparison. I'd stand on the docks for hours watching it sail past and Bill would tease: "Well, what are you waiting for? Does that stuff worry you? *Why?* It is nothing." And I'd say, "Oh. And what about that boat up in your workshop?" A cruiser with half the bottom torn out. To which Bill's reply would be a shrugged "Night driving. What do you expect?"

Fog had been adding another mournful touch to the general aspect, but fog and debris notwithstanding, towboats continued operating. As they slid past with massive unconcern, Bill would point and say, "There, he's going down. Nothing to worry about, you see. So when are you going?"

"I'll go when I'm ready. Stop bullying me."

Bill, of Germanic origin, with a fluent but not always exact command of English, looked puzzled: "Bulling — what's bulling?"

"Not bulling, for heaven's sake — bullying . . . nagging, Bill."

So later Bill would say, "I'm not *dogging* you, Ann, but when are you going?"

Bert kept saying the same sort of thing over the phone, the note of exasperation ringing louder each time we spoke ("Aren't you ever going to get out of that place?"), and one way and another, I was in a fine fluster of frustration.

There were a number of boats lying about the St. Louis waterfront waiting to go down the river, but few owners lived aboard. They lurked ashore in hotels, and were elusive and extremely cagy when tackled on departure plans. No whens or whys forthcoming at all.

One morning, without any prior ado, a small cruiser set out from the yacht docks, southward bound, in a thick fog, and I watched it disappear downstream with mixed feelings. *Was* it being foolhardy, as I thought, to go, or did I think that merely because I lacked the courage to do likewise?

Disconsolately I wandered down the dock to where Bill was talking to a tall, bulky man I had not seen before. "What on earth possessed them to go today, Bill?" the man was saying. "They might just as well have waited here, for they'll only have to stop at Cairo, if not before. The river's very high down there and still rising and the debris will be very bad. And they stand a good chance of being run down in this fog. If only they'd the patience to wait a few more days the river'll fall and be fit to travel. . . . I don't know what gets into people that they must go, go, go."

Such balm to the ego, such music to the ears. I planted myself in front of them, angling for an introduction with which Bill obliged, adding, "Mr. Patterson goes up and down the river every year. Anything you want to know about it, he can tell you." Which was what I thought.

Pat and Isabelle Patterson lived aboard a thirty-foot cruiser called the *Imp*, having taken to the water as a way of life after Pat's retirement from electrical engineering about four years previously. They were as ideal a couple as one could imagine, the product of a thirty-year marriage obviously cemented by friendship, respect and understanding, as well as love. They were two people so harmoniously complementary it was a pleasure to be with them, if only to have some of their restfulness brush off on you. A state all too rare. Most marriages seem to bog down in apathy, or survive, happy on a technical point, by the dominance of one of the partners (in which case you catch some of the tension).

The Pattersons came from South Dakota, where the *Imp* was registered (and so depicted on the stern, to the astonishment of the few more knowledgeable — geographically speaking — boatmen), but their home port was at St. Paul on the upper Mississippi. Every fall they sailed down from there to New Orleans, where they spent the winter, migrating north again along with the birds in the spring. Last spring they had gone home the long way round, across the Gulf of Mexico, the state of Florida and up the eastern seaboard to the Great Lakes — in fact making *my* trip and just ahead of me — but taking the Lake Erie route where I took the Trent.

It was refreshing to meet people completely unhampered by any of the prevailing status symbols and self-sufficient enough to be able to keep pretty much to themselves (which was why I hadn't seen them around, of course). Their approach to cruising was one of professional exactitude. They shared the running of the boat and kept her as shipshape as would delight the heart of the most carping old shellback. I don't know whether Pat had ever been a sailing man, but he had the manner of one.

"Of course it gets better," he had said when I posed my river question to him on the dock. "Certainly it will pay you to wait. Why don't you come round to the boat for River Stages tonight about six — we listen to the stages every night on ship-to-shore. . . . And bring your river chart so we can give you a run-down on the journey to New Orleans — there aren't many places you can get gas on the way down, and you could easily pass them up, if you don't know where to look for them."

River Stages, I discovered, are just that, stages of levels of the river, broadcast every evening for the benefit of river users. The level had fallen at points above us. At St. Louis the level was unchanged; farther downriver it was still rising.

"Won't be long now," said Pat. "It will be down here tomorrow, from the sound of it. Then we'll have to wait for it to fall quite a way ahead of us, otherwise we'd only catch up with the flood. Another two or three days and we should be able to start before it begins to rise again."

"Traveling between floods, as it were?"

"Yes. Now let's go over the chart. Isabelle, bring out your little black book."

Isabelle produced the book in which she meticulously

recorded journey data, times and distances between ports, gas consumption, alterations to markers, lights, buoys, etc., and as we went over the whole journey down to New Orleans, I marked my chart with pertinent and, as I was to find out, invaluable information.

Altogether it was an illuminating evening, and I felt much better about everything after it. Now I knew what I was waiting *for,* I didn't mind another two or three days. It was so simple, too, when one *knew*—what beats me is why it was all such a top secret.

iii

ONE hears so much about the Mississippi I was sure I was going to hate every minute of it, that it would be long streaks of nothing, interspersed, where civilization had struck, with Huck Finn Gift Shops and Mark Twain Pizza Palaces, so I was amazed and delighted by the river's extraordinary natural beauty and the almost total absence of tourism.

The vast Mississippi capillary water system drains forty per cent of the United States and 13,000 square miles of Canada, which is a lot of water and makes the Lower Mississippi, where it finally collects, into a truly impressive river. It has an entity of its own and character in the way the sea has — and a similar potential for catastrophe. It flows in all directions, like a snake twisting and winding north, east and west to reach the sea, a thousand miles south of St. Louis, lengthening and contracting the distance as it changes course, cutting corners, creating new islands and demolishing old ones. An exact distance between any two points on the Mississippi can never be stated, for it changes all the time, and this in spite of constant warfare waged by the U. S. Army Corps of Engineers to keep the river within bounds. Miles of levees and numerous great dams have been, and are being, constructed, channels are constantly being dredged, and still the great alluvial river exerts its will with new courses and sand bars and, occasionally, an overwhelming cataclysm.

Small-boat pilotage on the Lower Mississippi is exacting. Few towns are accessible from the water, and of those that are, many are hard to find, being hidden away up creeks with almost invisible entrances. And even fewer of these towns still cater to the transient, or indeed any, boatman.

Overnight stops are governed by places where one can refuel, which in turn regulates the day's run, so that this may be anything from fifty to one hundred and fifty miles a day. But it is not possible to telescope the short runs into the longer ones; however early in the day you may arrive at a fueling point at the end of a short run, by the time you've found the man with the key to the gas pump, or organized for a gas truck to come down to the river, it is too late to go on. To travel at night with a small boat is simply asking for trouble. On the other hand, it is not the sort of river on which one can carry on until it is dark and then anchor or tie up alongside the bank. Where banks are revetted it is impossible to lie alongside, and where they are not it is dangerous to do so, the banks being high and having a propensity for toppling over. Towboats have been smothered by a fall of earth this way. To lie up in a cut-off or tributary is to risk stranding, perhaps for weeks, as the river may fall enough overnight to leave it high and dry. Similarly with beaching on sand bars or mud-banks.

To anchor a small boat where the current may be anything up to ten knots, carrying trees and islands and rafts of logs with it, is, to say the least, inadvisable.

It is simpler, safer, and a great saving of time for the stranger in a small boat to follow the rules on the Mississippi. Stop at regular stopping places and travel in daylight only.

Between St. Louis and New Orleans there are nine stopping places. Of these, three have adequate dockage facilities, whilst the others have little or nothing, maybe only an extremely limited accessibility to the nearest town. If it hadn't been for the Pattersons' inside knowledge and their generous sharing of it, I might have been looking for some of those places yet, despite the charts.

The chart of the Lower Mississippi is a noble production, a book incorporating 62 maps, 12 charts, and 38 sheets of detailed instructional data. It is prepared annually, as it says on the front cover, "in the office of the President, Mississippi River Commission," which evokes a charming picture; cost $2.50 and worth every cent. I would hate to tackle the river without it, but quite apart from its undoubted navigational value, to a confirmed map-reader like myself it is an endless source of joy. The maps are beautifully prepared and look like old prints, but, to the uninitated, tend to make things appear rather more straightforward than they are. Towns that would appear to be right on the water turn out to be nonexistent, for all practical purposes. They hide behind steep levees and impregnable forests of sentinel pines, without so much as a rowboat landing to betray their presence. One of these hidden towns, in

Louisiana, is called Waterproof. There is such a triumphant ring about the name I wondered if there was a story attached to it. But when I got down that way I discovered the place was too darn waterproof for me to get near enough to find out.

When at last the all-clear was sounded at St. Louis, the river had fallen to a respectable level, the debris was comparatively scant, and there was no fog, I set out for the first stop—Cape Girardeau, 127 miles down the line—and hit a submerged log when within only a few miles of my destination.

Never saw the thing, was lolloping along quite happily, when suddenly *whang! wallop!* and *Gemini* was limping on one motor with a sore prop.

It was exasperating, as this was the first bent prop of the whole journey and it spoilt the set. I had hoped to make it a hole in one, so to speak, but it was not to be. Fortunately it was no worse and there wasn't far to go.

I tied up at a small dock with a fuel pump about half a mile north of the town, new, according to the Pattersons, who came in a little later, and a vast improvement, they said, over the old arrangement that used to obtain at the town itself, and which, so far as we could make out through the binoculars, no longer existed. It turned out that this dock belonged to a burgeoning boat club and later in the evening, when they had finished their day's work, members turned out in force to make us welcome and were most helpful and hospitable.

Next morning there was fog again, so thick I could hardly see the motors from the cabin six feet away, but it cleared by half past eight for a perfectly lovely day and as there was only a short run of fifty-five miles to the next stop, Cairo, there was no anxiety attached to making a late start.

Conditions were perfect, bright and clear with no wind, so that the water was calm and the driving easy. Debris was plain to see, which it is not when the surface is broken by ripples or waves, and the good clear light made it easier to pick out distant markers, lights and buoys.

It is essential to keep track of these and tick them off on the chart as you pass. If you don't, the river landscape, being repetitious and strangely featureless in its beauty, loses and disorients you so that you go aground or miss a vital turning.

Binoculars are a necessity for pilotage, for the river is wide and the reaches are long. The river wanders and the channel wanders in the river. Markers are several miles apart, and only with binoculars can they be discovered at times when the river is, say, two miles wide and five miles long on a particular reach. The courses and channels are so changeable that markers are not necessarily in the exact spot depicted on the chart. Many a time I stopped on a long reach to scan the distant horizon with binoculars for a marker, the mariner's signpost, to see which way to go.

I found that I had to drive with the top down, kneeling up on the pilot seat to look over the top of the windshield in order to get the best possible view. With *Gemini* scooting downstream at anything up to thirty miles an hour, it was wildly exhilarating, but cold and, after several hours, tiring, for there was absolutely no letup singlehanded.

"I don't know how you do it," Isabelle Patterson used to say. "It takes *both* of us all our time. . . ."

"And neither of us gets to see much of the scenery," added Pat with a grin. He drove and watched the water for debris and Isabelle navigated.

It was as well that we were in no hurry to get to Cairo, because we began to catch up with the flood. There were log jams at every bend to be navigated with care, and many of the channel buoys were drowned. Some of them were barely visible, only the tip of the nun and the horns of the can showing above water, and some of them were not visible at all. One knew they were there by a curious swelling on the surface of the water, and this would have been hidden by the slightest disturbance. These buoys are of colossal dimensions and to hit one at speed, which one could do by merely drifting with the current, would be well-nigh disastrous for a small boat.

Cairo (pronounced *Cay*ro by the inhabitants, who shy away at any other sound) lies, well bulkheaded against inundation, on a sliver of land between two mighty rivers, the Mississippi and the Ohio. In contrast to the fluid mud of the Mississippi, the Ohio has beautiful Bahama-clear water, and the two rivers meet to flow side by side, thick and thin, distinctly demarcated, for several miles before agreeing to mingle.

Cairo docks, a beat-up collection of old boats and

barges, somewhat intermittently run at that time by scouts, lay a mile or two up the Ohio River. We arrived there about midday, but it wasn't until evening that we managed to trap someone into unlocking the fuel pump, which incidentally leaked in a most unnerving manner.

It was pure pleasure to look down into crystal-clear water once more and see fish swimming about below, but it wasn't for long. Next day we were back in the mud again. Rough mud too, so that it took six hours for *Gemini* to thresh out the next leg, 114 miles to Caruthersville.

The Caruthersville boat docks were not at the town (one of the oldest river towns, and walled like a mediaeval castle); they lay up a small offshoot of the river that joined it obliquely, and I would most certainly have missed it but for the Pattersons' explicit directions. In fact, that evening, three boats I knew to be going south and undoubtedly expecting to stop over at Caruthersville went sailing past the end of the creek, plainly oblivious (it being one of those cases where it is easier to see out than in) of its presence and the harbor therein. By then there were three boats at the dock, which was a small floating platform secured to the shore by wire cables. One of those boats was a fifty-foot cruiser, longer than the dock, and she had the "inside" berth. Outside her lay the *Imp*, and *Gemini* was tucked in at one end of the dock, nosing the shore. Plainly the dock was already outnumbered. So we watched those boats go by and never so much as gave a toot on the horn to attract their attention. I had discovered in St. Louis that boatmen going downriver were reluctant to divulge the secrets of dockage. Now I knew why.

Mind you, the boats were not utterly abandoned to the mercies of the river. There are always tugs, barges or something of that nature lying about near towns, and it is tacitly understood on the river that you may at your own risk tie up to anything you can find.

Often, nowhere near a town, one comes across barges that have been dumped from one tow and are lying at anchor waiting to be picked up by another—a water-borne shunting operation. But they cannot be relied on to be *where* you want them *when* you want them, nor to stay where they are overnight. Boatmen have awakened in the morning to find themselves being carried back along the course they covered the day before because they did not know—and why should they?—the schedules of their temporary berths.

I liked the story of a yacht skipper who, trapped in a fog, happened on a couple of barges parked this way and thankfully made fast to them. He spent a restful night reasonably assured that the barges would not be moved in the fog; and then in the morning, finding the fog still thick, he switched on the ship-to-shore for the forecast and a run-down on what the towboat skippers had to say (usually this is plenty). He was amazed to hear himself called, and was even more amazed when, after he had responded, a towboat skipper inquired with a chuckle, "Since when, Captain, have you been in the towing business?"

The barges had broken loose overnight, and with the

yacht alongside had been drifting down the river for hours. . . .

Ship-to-shore, about which there's a fairly acid school of thought in some places ("yakking sons-of-bitches, you can't get a word in edgewise," I heard one disgruntled pot complaining of the kettles on Gulf waters) appears to be a valuable adjunct to pleasure-boat operating on the Mississippi. The Pattersons used theirs extensively to keep informed regarding conditions, floods, fogs, location and extent of debris. They also like to know the whereabouts of towboats in order to avoid meeting them or following them in narrow cutoffs or chutes (places where the river, frequently assisted by the Engineers, has chewed through a loop and saved itself several miles). Where there were locks, the Pattersons would call up the lock-tender and find out the situation there so that they could adjust their speed of approach accordingly and avoid a long wait at the gates.

Much of their river information came through listening to towboat skippers talking among themselves. These conversations were entertaining as well as instructive, for like any specialized business, the river towing fraternity has a language of its own. Graphically referring to their barges they talk about "coming up the river lightheaded," or "carrying one on the hip."

It is customary for boats to salute one another in passing on the river, as it is for people in most places where there aren't too many of them, but for the first few days I thought the towboats were rather overdoing it in the extravagance of their address. "Well, I love you too," I thought waving an inadequate response to all the tooting and song and dance that went on aboard a passing tow.

Then I discovered that a yacht skipper who knew of my present venture and some of my past ones was also making the downstream passage and passing the time en route recounting these adventures over the air. Pretty graphically, too, judging by the interested reaction. The Pattersons unwittingly added fuel to the small fire by inquiring from time to time my whereabouts from northbound tows — *Gemini* being the faster boat.

Well, well, a lone seagoing woman! What next! *Gemini* became a marked boat, rating instant recognition from passing vessels and at each place she put into. Not having ship-to-shore, I was mystified until I found out the reason, and then it was like being deaf at a party, or watching television with the sound turned off (though the latter is vastly improved thereby, in my opinion).

At Memphis, the next stop after Caruthersville and 120 miles farther on the way, the press seemed actually to be lying in wait. I'd barely got the boat tied up when a representative of the local paper pounced. Inundated under an encyclopedic deluge of local statistics, I was swept away to see the sights, feeling fraudulent because I was obviously expected to make use of the information. But I have no affinity at all for facts and figures in the raw state.

We drove round the town and saw its lovely parks, and into the country to listen to the nerve-shattering din of cotton mills and look at the fields where plants were stuck about with tufts of cotton looking absurdly like what it is. Then we drove to a hilltop and looked down on the spacious new harbor. Since it is miles out of town, it won't be as handy for the traveling boatman as the present boat dock, which is literally at the foot of the town. Finally we drove to the newspaperman's home, nestling in trees beside a lake. His wife graciously extended the hospitality of her washing machine, a gesture guaranteed to fix any place in a boat traveler's memory.

I like Memphis. I thought it was the most handsome town on the Lower Mississippi, which isn't much of a recommendation, considering the appearance of most river towns. But as a matter of fact, Memphis could hold its own in any metropolitan company. It has a spacious air, and the streets sparkle as if they had been scoured and polished but a moment before. It is a civic-minded, proud and hospitable town, a civil and accommodating place in which to have dealings, and I was really sorry to see that it too had fallen prey to the subdivision.

This menace of our time, one of its most destructive forces, has not abated one whit since it was so brilliantly pointed up by John Keats in *The Crack in the Picture Window.* On the contrary, it is spreading farther and farther afield. There wasn't a town I went through on this 6000-mile trip that wasn't in the strangle hold of suffocating suburbia. Even Peterborough in Canada was not immune. Unable, or unwilling, to see these developments for what they are — the perpetuation of false values and conformity, the death of individuality and cultural advancement—civically responsible people actually regarded them with pride.

However, if it ever gets too much for Memphis, the people there can always take to their boats, of which there is a tidy population of 16,000. Few, though, stray far from home.

It is very noticeable how strictly local boating remains on the river. Five miles away from a populous center and you are on your own. Even commercial vessels are few and far between. Huge freightage is transported on the Mississippi, but the eggs are not carried in many baskets. It was unusual to see more than three tows in a distance of 150 miles, and solitude was a striking feature of the Mississippi. Sometimes, though, a strange and interesting vessel made a lonely appearance.

Shortly after leaving Memphis I passed a stern-wheeler belonging to the Engineers. Paddle-boats are almost synonymous with the Mississippi, but few remain in operation. This one, I learned later, was the last of the Engineers' old-style boats, and it was her last working voyage. She went by, leaving a truly appalling wake that churned up the river for miles; but I was told that it was nothing to the one left by the *Sprague*. This giant stern-wheeler left in her wake a twelve-foot wash that had all the devastating properties of a tidal wave. She had been retired at public demand not too long ago, at the height of her career, and was moved to Vicksburg, where she was used for dockage purposes. "Dock," incidentally, is a word that is in the process of evolution and at a somewhat confusing stage. Strictly speaking, the word "dock" refers to an artificial basin or space for the reception of vessels, as, for instance, the waterway between two piers. Through popular usage the word has come to include in its meaning the piers, wharves and jetties that surround the "dock" proper. The *Sprague* retired to "become the docks" at Vicksburg, but that is not to say that she was liquidated!

Vicksburg was a town on my stopping list, and I looked forward to seeing the huge vessel — I understand her wheel was forty feet in diameter — but by the time I got to Vicksburg she had gone gallivanting off to some exhibition (*not* under her own power) and had not returned. All I saw was one of her tremendous rudders standing, a somewhat inconclusive monument, on top of the levee.

Excluding purely local outbreaks near towns, yachts and pleasure-boats were limited to the convoys released by sporadic breaks in the weather and forced to travel south at the same time, though not necessarily together. They comprised the usual hodgepodge of humanity that goes to make up any small community. There were the big shots, aloof in their great cruisers; small shots in small, overloaded, underpowered boats; the status-seekers with a new and bigger boat, assiduously avoiding those who had been on the river with them before and knew them when; the nice guys, the goons and the bores; and the mystery. Actually our mystery was not noticeably mysterious to begin with, and later it was really rather more squalid than puzzling. But for a time it had us engrossed.

The boat involved was a medium-sized powerboat of

about thirty feet and unremarkable in every way; the kind you would never look at twice or remember. It was run by a couple who, aside from the fact that the female was larger and more deadly-looking than the male, were as unobtrusive as their boat. They were quietly sullen and kept to themselves.

Then early one morning the woman went galloping down the dock, brandishing a revolver and vowing to shoot the son-of-a-bitch.

As a way of getting attention this is practically unequaled, and she had all ours, undivided.

It seemed her husband had left her. On their honeymoon, yet. Three weeks married and he'd lit out that morning, "and he means it, the bastard, he's taken his tool-box," and there she was in the middle of nowhere with a boat she didn't know how to operate and no money. The picture of a jilted, lovelorn bride was somewhat marred by the construction of said bride, which was on the lines of a lady wrestler, and by the basso profundo delivery of the story in terms seldom heard outside a modern novel.

The metamorphosis of the lady wrestler after her husband disappeared lent credence to the rumor that she had swept him under the rug herself. Up to then she had scarcely spoken, now she never stopped. She departed from the dock that morning in a drab cocoon of dungarees and returned in the evening the butterfly product of the beauty parlor, wearing the tight skirt of the trade and stiletto heels sharp enough to slit a throat. There was nothing puny about this gal, nothing half-hearted. When she wept over her misfortunes she bawled at the top of her voice. When she drowned her sorrows she went on a bat that ranged over the countryside and lasted a week. Her ordinary conversation was defined in a manner that made the most red-blooded cusser among us sound like an amateur.

She put the boat up for sale, and thereafter a stream of sheepish red-necked young men arrived on the dock to be shown the boat, much, it was surmised, as a less sophisticated generation was shown etchings.

Sometimes the young man really wanted to see the boat and then there was a great to-do. If it didn't end in a flat battery, it entailed a riotous departure from the dock during which every boatman in the place appeared on his deck up to the neck in fenders and armed with a boathook. After the cruiser had ricocheted its way to open water the potential purchaser — and the pop-eyed watchers ashore — were treated to a demonstration the like of which people pay good money to see in a circus.

Up and down the river belted the poor old boat, flat out and bow high, with no regard for debris or traffic. The lady wrestler stood at the wheel spinning it the way they do in the movies, yelling *Yippee* as she blasted the horn, executing tight turns and fancy figure-eights which sent up a shower of spray like breakers on a half-tide rock and must have strained the hull to the final splinter.

Confusing her vehicles, she'd cut the throttles cold, as a motor salesman jams on the brakes to show how well the car stops short, then with a jerk that would throw the young man off his feet, she'd open up again and rocket off.

It was an exciting demonstration, but not noticeably conducive to sales.

In her metamorphosis the lady wrestler had shed her role of timid know-nothing-about-boats for the one of know-all salt, and some of the things she knew were quite fascinating.

As with the weather elsewhere, the level of the water is a constant source of comment on the river.

"It's gone down," someone said one morning, as one says "nice day" or "looks like rain," and the lady wrestler chipped in, "Kee-rist, it sure has," and pointing to the boarding ladder mounted on the stern of her boat, added, "Lookit that. Yesterday the son-of-a-bitch was way up over the middle step, now it's to hell and gone below the bottom one."

I must say she brightened our lot considerably. Fog lifting too late in the morning to allow of departure held us over for several days in the little river town, but thanks to the lady wrestler boredom was kept at bay. If her own antics were not enough there were always the rumors, and they were rife.

Her husband had vanished off the face of the earth, and dragging operations were to begin.

He had been seen in Chicago, Boston, St. Louis, New Orleans and the police had him right here in town.

She was asking anything from two to twenty thousand for that old hooker, forheavenssake.

Some sap had just bought it for nine.

Someone else had just got a bargain at six.

She couldn't sell it until the "papers" arrived (from any town in any state of the Union).

He had the papers.

There were no papers.

They weren't honeymooners, you know, they'd been married for *years.*

They were not married at all.

Well, she was well rid of him. You mean he was well rid of her. No, they were well rid of each other.

A clear morning dawned and I left before the case of the lady wrestler closed. I never knew how it came out but going the rounds at the time of my departure was a gorgeously juicy rumor that the whole thing was a Put-Up Job.

They had stolen the boat from some place way, way up north and sailed south until they found this place, sufficiently out of the way so that the boat would not be easily recognized, and where the locals, they figured, were uncomplicated enough not to be hep to their little drama — Must Sell Says Deserted Bride Low Price For Quick Sale. Then after the boat was sold the bride would decamp with the spoils to join — one hesitates to say — her lover.

Whatever the truth of the matter, the absence of ownership papers, or something, seemed to be proving a stumbling block in the way of any sale. Not perhaps that it mattered. When I left, the lady wrestler seemed to be making out all right. She was still showing the boat. . . .

iv

HELENA was the fifth stop on the Mississippi, the one after Memphis, and 73 miles nearer New Orleans. A small town with new and unusually good small-boat dockage — especially for the river — and the *Pelican.* Not the bird-whose-beak, but a ferryboat as proportionately capacious and just as implausible to look at. Helena's *Pelican* transported trains across the river. It was a sidewheeler of monumental proportions, exquisitely antique, faintly comic and all curlicues as if designed by Emmet or Ronald Searle. It moved with great dignity and quite extraordinary maneuverability in a silence that was broken at long and regular intervals by a sigh from its innermost being and an occasional incongruously thin, plaintive toot on its whistle.

Helena was a one-night stand and next morning I drove on to Greenville, passing en route two young men making the trip downriver in rubber tires. They each had two tires coupled together. The tires had canvas "decks"; one was to sit in and the other carried stores and equipment. According to newspaper reports, eventually they arrived safely at New Orleans. They had camped on sandbars at night, since it was impossible for them to stop anywhere except directly on the river.

Their sole motive power had been the current, and their only complaint was of the cold.

Greenville was one of those places that hide up insignificant-looking creeks, and I almost missed it. It was a most sociable town. Friends of friends bore down on the docks at my arrival to engulf me in a tide of Southern hospitality. We roared away for dinner, gathering strength and more friends on the way, and fetched up at Does.

Does was an old-fashioned eating place notable for its cooking and atmosphere. As part of the stock in trade it makes no concessions. What was good enough for granddad is good enough for grandson. People used to eat in the kitchen. People still do. It's a real old-style kitchen — but a working model, none of your false copper bottoms and stainless steel. Here the boards were bare, worn and bleached by time and scrubbing. An ironbound kitchen redolent of onion, raw meat and hot bread. Large overflowing women with big bare arms, girded in aprons, bustled in slow motion, complacently chopping, stirring and beating, impervious to the expectant, eager appetites about them.

The diners sit cheek by jowl at kitchen tables, and one feels faintly surprised at being given plates and cutlery in the usual way and slightly nettled at *not* being given the bowls to scrape out.

The food was excellent. It was a popular place, crowded and noisy. I go deaf in confusion, so I missed the merry quips flying around. One remark I caught throughout the dinner: "*Miami Beach*," said a voice of scorn, raised in an effort to surmount the clatter that had suddenly ceased momentarily, "nothing but Coney Island with rhinestones."

Southern hospitality extended to a fifty-five-mile drive to the friend's friends' house, a scaled-down version of a colonial mansion complete with columns. My host had retired from cotton to become a radio ham. A click of the switch and he was off on a communication spree, chattering with someone on the other side of the world or in the next room. Intercom in the home I found somewhat daunting. Voices that come out of the wall never fail to strike me dumb. I like to have a face attached to the voice that addresses me. Telephones are bad enough, but at least the phone gives one a focal point, as it were.

On the way back to the boat next morning we passed a minuscule Fiat trundling along with a notice on its back window reading "Help Stamp Out Cadillacs." ("Old stuff," said Bert when I told him of this on our next phone date. But it was new to me and I liked it.)

Greenville is in the heart of the Delta country, where cotton reigns and the atmosphere is just about as Deep South as you can get. The ghosts of Rhett and Scarlet die hard and every vowel is broken three ways. So it was amusing to learn that the biggest cotton operation thereabouts was run by a group of Manchester men. What wouldn't I have given to hear those two rich accents together!

I don't believe it is generally realized how strong the English infiltration is into the U.S. I was always running into my fellow countrymen and women, behind the scenes, quietly digging themselves in, as is their wont. It was "that time" again for a story, so I stayed in Greenville for a few days to write it and used to have afternoon tea with an Englishman and his American wife, Dick and Libby Goodwin. Dick was an ex-RAF fighter pilot turned cotton planter. He would come bounding up to the boat at three o'clock saying, "How about a cupper?" and whisk me back to the farm, where Libby would prepare tea. We'd sit around our teacups exchanging news and views and building up a small stockpile of energy with which to resume the day's chores.

A bridge had been constructed fairly recently across the river, and made such a difference to local travel that the people of Greenville looked on it with the fond pride usually reserved for personal animate property. Dick drove me by to see it and as we drove across said triumphantly, "No toll, you see. It's paid for itself by carrying the gas pipes across. Nearly lost it one night though, by gum, Just after it was opened. Clot in a jet tried to fly under and pranged it. Blew the pipes, nearly pitched the whole works off its pedestals, and set it on fire. But we managed to save it in time."

If they hadn't, I reckon Greenville would have gone into mourning.

Dick and Libby had two small children, a boy of three and an almost brand-new girl. The children had arrived after fourteen years of marriage, and it was a wonderfully happy household. "Having children while you're young," meaning while you are one yourself almost, has become axiomatic, and any suggestion to the contrary is met with the argument that it is more natural to have children when you're young. Any argument that drags in nature in connection with humanity is in danger of being invalid from the start. It would be natural for many girls to reproduce at nine years old, but it is not necessarily desirable. Theoretically, people in their thirties should make better parents than those in their twenties. Life is very complex for the human animal and growing more so. And it takes longer for people to mature emotionally; they have that much more to learn. There might be a chance of older parents having acquired greater tolerance, wisdom, guidance ability, and, with their own security more assured, a vastly increased capacity for selfless loving, which are the things children surely need from parents.

As it is, we have people, still children themselves, often still at school, their futures uncertain, their values confused, inexperienced, malleable, gullible, subconsciously scared out of their wits, charged with the tremendous responsibility of raising children. It is true they have time to raise *more* children, but it is yet to be proved where quantity has it over quality. Humanity, supremely egotistical, seems bent on improving everything but itself. At least up to now. But there's hope. The birth control pills, which have come into being with less fanfare and comment than that caused by the slipping décolletage of a third-rate television performer, have the greatest potential of anything yet devised for benefiting humanity as a whole. They might even save it. . . .

Greenville is another one of those highly individualistic Mississippi towns full of artists, writers and poets.

There was dinner one night with the Hodding Carters, though I did not know with whom it was going to be when I accepted the invitation. Out of the blue, so far as I was concerned, Betty Carter called me up at the Yacht Club. My writing had not gone well that day, I was tired and cross when I went to the phone, I didn't catch her name, and if I'd been quick enough I would have said no, thank you. But for once I was grateful for a tardy reaction. It was a most rewarding evening, one of those after which, though little is recalled of what has been said, there's an agreeable feeling of mental expansion.

Hodding Carter, the publisher and author, and his charming wife Betty were recently returned from an African tour and full of jungle lore. Lions lurked behind sofas, baboons swung on the drapes, and giraffes peered over the rooftop. To intensify the African atmosphere they had as house guests a young couple, newlyweds, from South Africa, here in the States studying the newspaper business. The young South Africans were a delightful pair, wearing their youth and enthusiasm with a most refreshing grace and charm. After dinner we were joined by Byrne Keating and his wife and the conversation swung to writing, photography and allied arts. Talk that was rare enough for me, as writing per se is of necessity a solitary occupation, and my active life usually takes me into areas where the creative arts have no part and are practically unknown. My ears were spread like batwings. And what have I to report? Nothing. All that remains of that evening is the memory of a gentle euphoria that follows mental stimulation. The tug of ambition . . . the dream of the book one would write one day . . . the picture one would paint. The world one would set afire . . .

Hodding Carter, off next morning on another foray, offered the use of his study in which to finish my story. "Come and see it," he said. "You wouldn't need to bring your typewriter even, everything's there. All you'd need would be your notes."

But one glance at the study and I knew it wouldn't do. Not only could I not work there but I would not even be able to leave the place until I had read all the books in it. Floor to ceiling, on all four walls, barely leaving room for windows and doors, the walls were lined with shelves loaded with beautiful books. And as if that was not bad enough, there were fine, deep, comfortable chairs in which to read them.

One morning the young South African stopped by the boat. He was curious to see *Gemini,* and I of course was curious to hear about conditions in South Africa, of which he spoke more sadly than bitterly, though bitter was more his lot. His father was Greek and his mother English, parentage which would hardly seem disadvantageous even for that bigoted country. Nevertheless it closed many doors and opportunities to him, and put him low in the pecking order.

Surely the most terrible feature of human nature is its apparent inability to overcome its basic insecurity; people seem to be able to survive only at each other's expense, their own surety being dependent upon another's subordination. Man forever sets himself against man, racially and sexually, white and colored, man and woman, in a ceaseless desperate striving for the upper hand.

The condition of subordination is something no human being should ever be required to accept *by virtue of birth alone*. People are to a great extent what other people make them, and the problem lies not so much in educating the oppressed as in educating the oppressors.

So long as this condition exists, one that is based entirely on the assumption that might is right, there can be no peace anywhere in the world. And until there is a universal peace it is futile for the exponents of different "ways of life" to claim theirs — as they all do — as being the "right" one. Just how "right" it is for the individual depends on where he happens to have been placed by the accident of his birth in the pecking order, at the top of which stands today, supreme, but a little rocky, the Protestant white man.

If the human individual per se is of no importance, then what, may I ask, is?

V

A VISIT to the Greenville Quarterboats was n interesting side trip and came about through the Petersons, who had had occasion on one of their trips to seek shelter with a Greenville Quarterboat when it wasıt work on the river. They spent several days with *Imp* tied up alongside and had been most royally entertaind. After which they never passed through the area withut visiting the Boats, whether they (the Boats) were in Greenville or on the river. This time, knowing I woud be interested, they took me along.

A quarterboat is an operational center for the maintenance and repair department of the U.S. Army Corps of Engineers, Mississippi River Commission, the boys that keep Ol' Man River from getting out of bounds. Quarterboats are stationed at various pints on the river covering a designated area and are veritable townships of boats. There were three at Greenille and they could be moved as a whole or in individal units as the nature of the work required. Each boatis completely self-contained and able to stay out on a job indefinitely. On board there are complete living quarters and repair shops, along with water-making andelectrical parts. Each boat has its own work and communication boats, and at least $60,000 worth of spares. The crews are proud of their work, with every right. The Engineers have not succeeded in completely subduing the Mississippi, but they've got it pretty well crying "uncle" compared with the days when it used to go on the rampage, at times reaching a width of eighty miles. And of course navigational hazards for river users have been so immeasurably reduced that even a tire can use it!

The Greenville Yacht Club had good docks, the usual floating type, and many of the slips were covered, their pitched roofs and straight sides making them look like rows of little arks. *Imp* and *Gemini* were berthed in the open but comfortably sheltered.

"Make the most of it here," warned Pat, "these are the last docks until we get to New Orleans. From now on it's a question of finding something to tie up to and God knows what we'll find at Vicksburg now they've moved the *Sprague*."

What we found was the most astonishing floating junkyard imaginable.

Every old boat, barge, boiler, cable, crankcase, crane and drum in the neighborhood, whole or in part, seemed to have been dumped higgledy-piggledy at the bottom of the levee, as if someone had started a scrap heap there and on being challenged had said quickly, "Why, that's the Vicksburg Yacht Club," and got away with it.

Tying up to it wasn't so bad, but getting across it to go ashore entailed a lot of goatlike crag-to-crag agility. There were all manner of obstacles and pitfalls. Differing levels, (disguised) gaps, open hatches, loops of electrical cable and twisted wire, protruding handles and sharp edges.

The dockmaster was a gentle wraith of a man with tufts of white hair peeping out from under his hat. "What's *she* up to?" he asked Pat as he watched me. "Is she writing a book?"

Pat, a firm believer that everyone's business is his own, said he didn't know, to which the dockmaster replied significantly, "She will, you'll see. They all do."

Vicksburg, a very vertical town, towers over a narrow tributary of the Mississippi, the Yazoo (to which the only possible comment is yazoo to you, too), and it is the most difficult place in which to find a grocery store. When you do, it is practically out in the country and called, not inappropriately on account of this, the Jitney Jungle.

The run down from Greenville had been made in lovely weather, calm and *hot*. It was the first time in weeks I had driven without a top coat and I began to feel I was really making progress south. A fairly fleeting feeling, for the following morning in Vicksburg dawned with every sign of a blow and bad weather, and sure enough, before long a whomping wind came barreling up from the south with all the trappings of boating misery: squalls, showers and head seas. Even the tiny Yazoo had to get into the act. Six-inch waves tumbled up the river sporting baby crests, minutely fierce like a growling puppy. Over the *Imp*'s ship-to-shore we heard towboat skippers complaining of having to slow right down and decided the river was no place for us.

"It may not be much here," said Isabelle, "but at least it is sheltered."

"The last we'll have," said Pat. "When we leave here we must be sure of our weather; there's no protection at any of the gas stops until we get to New Orleans now."

Two days of this and then the dark oppression that had given us all cabin fever lifted. In high good humor we got ready and set out.

The Mississippi as it nears the sea slows down, and the reduced current is brought home to the boatman in an apparent increase in fuel consumption, often discovered the hard way.

Bulkheads called wing dams, similar to groins on a beach, make their appearance on this part of the river and are to be watched for, as they extend far out into the water with their ends frequently submerged.

The word "wing-dam" swung happily in my brain as *Gemini* droned along. I thought it would make a useful addition to my personal stock of cusswords. For satisfactory cussing, the meaning of a word is not so important as the rhythm of it and the amount of feeling one can put in its audible expression, and you can really slam the door with *wing-dam!* "Hot tamales" has a good swing, but is more surprised than mad.

The two possible stops between Vicksburg and New Orleans are at Natchez and Baton Rouge.

Natchez, visible from the river, stands on the left

bank (going south) and faces Vidalia, not visible from the river, on the other side. Neither town had any boating facilities, but the Pattersons recommended Vidalia from previous experience.

"There may be a pipe-laying barge to tie up to," said Pat before we set out, "and it is easier to get a gas truck there than at Natchez."

The pipe-laying barge was there, along with a tugboat. They were so arranged that it was possible for us to lay our boats alongside and inshore of them, thereby gaining a measure of protection.

The Pattersons — my friends at court — were roundly welcomed by the pipe-laying crew — "Heck, you're *late,* thought you were never coming" — who whistled up a gas truck in no time.

Having no idea what constituted a "gas truck" in these circumstances, I had been very curious about this operation. I vaguely imagined a van full of forty-gallon drums from which the fuel would somehow have to be decanted into our boat tanks. The gas truck turned out to be one of those big tankers that take care of filling stations. I don't know why it hadn't occurred to me that they might also be obliging enough to take care of boats. Although our boats lay on the shore side of the barge, they were too far away, even when the truck was backed to the very edge of the marl and gravel bank, for the hose to be simply handed across from the tanker. The hose was ferried across in a small skiff to each of our boats in turn, and refueling was accomplished with very little trouble.

The weather, with its usual treachery, dropped the mercury almost out of sight overnight, and made the drive to Baton Rouge next day the coldest one of the trip. It was also very rough, but it was too cold to matter. Unheeding of the brutal jolting or the blinding upshoots of spray I drove flat out to Baton Rouge in a furious effort to get there and end the misery.

If service is a measure of welcome, small boats are not wanted in Baton Rouge — small boats in this case being pleasure boats of almost any size. And in truth they have no place there, for Baton Rouge is a busy port, a seaport in fact, and full of seagoing vessels. Steamers from Panama and South America, from across the Caribbean, the Atlantic and the Gulf, lie at anchor in the middle of the broad brown river, incongruous in an inland setting. But there is nowhere else for a smallboatman to stop, and since he must stop, he has to make the best of Baton Rouge and pay highly for the privilege.

Dockage charges in the Deep South, along the Mississippi and in Gulf ports along the Mississippi and Alabama coasts, appear to be on an inverse scale to the facilities offered. The fewer, the higher. Outraged boatowners could be heard breast-beating any morning of departure: "Charged me five bucks to lie alongside his old junkpile for one night, for Chrissake!" Personally I cannot complain, for I found dock rates for *Gemini* very reasonable. Often they were waived altogether: "Can't charge you anything for that little boat, she don't take up no room." But whilst appreciating the gesture for its kindness and financial saving, I found it was apt to put me in the somewhat invidious position of "teacher's pet" among my fellow boatmen.

A floating boat store at Baton Rouge, commissary for the provisioning of towboats and ships, granted berthing privileges to transient pleasure boats. The store consisted of several steel barges linked together to form a long-backed L, the long part being parallel to the river with the base pointing toward the shore. Luckily for us the water was still high so that *Imp* and *Gemini* were able to creep round the end of the L and lie on the inshore side, well protected. At normal water level, we would have had to lie outside in the turbulent stream. Tugboats lay there, three and four abreast, nodding and weaving, grinding against one another's heavy matting fenders. A tall, thin tugboat with a list and the name *Felicity Ann* evoked many memories, and a colossal black glossy pig on one of the barges belonging to the store, some surprise.

The store had no facilities for refueling. This we accomplished on the morning of departure for New Orleans at an Esso barge, a mobile fueling unit for big ships, which carried a few drums of "light" fuel on deck, purely as a courtesy for traveling boatmen. Home base for this barge lay about three quarters of a mile downriver from the floating store, but there was no guarantee that it would be there when wanted. Usually one fills the tanks on arrival, but it had been too cold on that run down from Vidalia to even consider such a thing. It was such a vital matter, and at Baton Rouge so uncertain, that we watched the Esso barge like hawks. Hawks with binoculars, ready to descend on him at the first sign of movement.

By nighttime he was still there, but when two more cruisers tied up at the store, Pat got really restive.

"We'll have to get down to that barge, if he's there in the morning, as soon as it's light. He doesn't carry much in those drums, and there won't be enough for those guys as well."

Next morning the barge was still there. We lost no time in getting down to him and between us cleared out every single drum of fuel. Early predatory birds.

The run from Baton Rouge to the yacht basin on Lake Pontchartrain, New Orleans, the final one on the Mississippi, was 140 miles and a tax on *Gemini*'s gasoline resources, leaving little margin for head winds or any other adversities. However, there was no way of getting any en route without considerable brouhaha. I did not anticipate running out before the lock on the Inner Harbor Canal in New Orleans — the turnoff for Lake Pontchartrain — but Pat said, "Well, if you do, we can always give you a tow."

The main tanks ran out on the outskirts of New Orleans. I switched to the emergency tanks (roughly an hour's running and roughly an hour to go) and slowed down to wait for the *Imp*. I was not far from the Inner Harbor Canal Lock, which had a reputation for keeping small boats waiting a long time — Pat said they had waited there for as long as four hours. I thought two boats might look more urgent to the lock-keeper than one, and anyway now that *Gemini* was running on her emergency tanks I did not want to be far away from the *Imp*.

Luck was with us at the lock, for we got the green light on sight. Already in the basin was a tugboat that seemed enormous beside our little boats, and the lock-master instructed us to make fast alongside her for locking.

The tugboat captain looked at *Gemini* and then at me and said, "I know you. Last time I saw you was in New York Harbor. You had a sailboat then. I was in the Coast Guard — radio — and received the message of your arrival."

Gemini, having bottomless tanks apparently, made the yacht harbor under her own steam with a few gallons to spare; and the long ride down the Mississippi was over.

Journey's end always gives me a hollow feeling, a sense of loss. A journey becomes a part of one, a little life with its own triumphs and defeats, problems, special associations and allusions, a compact version of the real thing. I felt this more about the Mississippi than about any other section of the voyage, or even the voyage as a whole, partly because the conditions peculiar to the river made it an experience apart, and partly because of Pat and Isabelle Patterson.

We had not at any point decided to travel together; the fact that we did was the result of a similar approach to cruising which brought us to the same place more or less at the same time. And because of the similarity in our attitudes, we began to look out for each other more and more, so that our friendship grew and developed into one of those easygoing, undemanding associations that are so enriching without ever being enervating.

The Pattersons "made" the Mississippi for me. By sharing their hard-won knowledge of the river, they made my jaunt down it very much simpler than it might have been, but quite apart from that, I enjoyed them so. They were two of the nicest people I've ever met.

New Orleans is at the end of a line. Anything, so long as it can stay afloat, will find its way eventually down the Mississippi, and only too often, anything does. But the current runs out at New Orleans, and frequently the money does, too, and many an ill-begotten venture founders there. New Orleans shares with Gibraltar and Panama the dubious distinction of being a graveyard for dreams — and dreamboats.

Consequently the New Orleans Yacht Harbor is wary of strangers, any strangers, and it doesn't matter what they arrive in. As a defense against having the slips filled with abandoned hulks, dockage at the harbor is not readily available and prices are high.

Here, then, for the last time Pat and Isabelle waved their influential wand for me. I sailed in under their colors, as it were, and as they were known of old and *personae gratae* with the harbormaster, *Gemini* was allowed to lie, for a very reasonable fee, cater-corner at the end of the slip allotted to the *Imp*.

[illegible] of the same people [illegible]

[illegible] Christians, and the [illegible]

[illegible]

PART FIVE

Gulf

i

ONCE upon a time, when you went away on a long journey your good-byes were for the duration, and everyone at home figured you were a memory until you returned. Now you can set off for the other side of the world and break the journey at any point on the way and be home in a matter of hours, popping up through a trap door in time to give the home folks fits. What is more, you can put the whole thing into reverse, drop out of sight again and take up the journey where you left off, repeating the operation as often as you like — and the money holds out. But it feels like cheating.

At New Orleans I left the boat and flew home. The reason for leaving the trip in abeyance was the arrival of my sister Jo from England, on her first visit to the U.S. The visit was first planned for the spring before I left with *Gemini*. But Jo and her husband have three children and a farm in Wales, factors that influence one's plans no end, and eventually the visit was postponed until November. At that time I hadn't started on the trip, so of course I would be home by then. Of course. In Chicago I had begun to be doubtful about this, and in St. Louis I was pretty darn sure I wouldn't be home; but by then I stopped worrying about it. So I wouldn't be home. So why shouldn't Jo join me on the trip and take a *Gemini*-view too? This course was agreed upon through a complicated three-way discussion between Jo, Bert and myself via airmail and telephone.

The day before Jo arrived there had been a record rainfall in Miami of eleven inches, and as water hasn't much place to go in south Florida there was still plenty of it lying about.

"Eleven inches!" cried Jo, a touch accusingly. "Why, we don't have that much in a year at home!"

"Ah," said Bert, "but we like to get it all over at once here."

There are certain things — children, gardens, fish and the weather — about which bragging is irresistible, acceptable and yet half-believed — and which as a consequence rarely live up to their false reputations. My letters to Jo had always been full of the basking quality of the Florida climate. "All you'll need in the way of clothes when you come over will be shorts and swim suits," I used to write, and the weather promptly let me down by staging this spectacular rainfall. Jo knew that the boat was in New Orleans, but had heard that New Orleans was in the Deep South. "South" for the English means somewhere where it is warm in winter, so my sister arrived with a suitcase full of shorts and swimsuits and we left at once for Louisiana, where it is decidedly cold in winter.

Jo could stay for three weeks, and we decided to spend roughly two weeks on the boat, getting as far as possible, and the last week at home.

As Jo's arrival coincided with a weekend, Bert drove

us over to Tampa, on the west coast of Florida, dallying on the way for Jo to see something of the palm tree state. It was Sunday night when we rolled into the airport at Tampa to enplane for New Orleans and very nearly midnight by the time we rolled aboard the little boat at the yacht basin.

Jo and I were both "only" children, in that she is twelve years younger than I and there is no one between or on either side of us. Either because of or in spite of this we have always got along extremely well. Jo is the stable one. She consolidates where I dib and dab. She picks up where I let fall. She has dark brown hair, melting brown eyes, a peaches complexion in spite of an outdoor life, and never looks a day over twenty-five. Jo is the most equable person I know and quite one of the best to have along on a ploy.

She had not done any small-boat cruising before but started right in that night with the contortions attendant on outboard living, merely remarking that it was cozy.

And that it was. We slept on either side of the cabin, sardine fashion. The one on the starboard side had to sleep foreshortened with feet in the forepeak, tangled up in the anchor line, and head against the sink. We underwent this in turns. For more than one person aboard, small-boat living is an alternate thing. Everything is done in turns—and you don't pull sweaters over your heads at the same time.

From first to almost last the weather on our trip was appalling. Fog, dripping and penetrating, delayed us in New Orleans for a day. "Humph," said Jo, borrowing a pair of my slacks. We spent the day dragging the stores for cans of heat to keep the stove going and the cabin warm. (For some reason we could not plug in the electric stove. Probably the extension cord was too short. As the journey progressed and the cold intensified, this was remedied to such an extent that by the time I eventually returned to Miami with *Gemini* I could have hooked up to an outlet a block away.)

Three things about New Orleans struck us: the extraordinary lack of mail boxes, five-cent phone calls and the remarkable public transportation (remarkable because it was there, it covered most of the sprawling town and it was very cheap—seven cents to the end of the line). Jo of course liked the dime stores, and the supermarkets too, but they weren't specifically New Orleans.

Next morning the fog blew away on the wind, taking with it any hope of making a calm passage. Lake Pontchartrain was rough, but we set out all the same, only to have to give up after a few miles. We did not have to turn back, but turned off into the Industrial Canal which also leads out into the Gulf, or rather that portion of it known as the Mississippi Sound. About halfway along the twenty-mile canal we stopped at a small shipyard for commercial fishing vessels, tucked away in a lay-by alongside a bridge. We switched on the transistor radio to find out what was going on in the weather department and were informed hoarsely that small-craft warnings were flying from Brownsville, Texas, to St. Marks, Florida. Which at least made the condition pretty general.

The Industrial Canal appears to be named ambitiously. At present the only thing in the way of industry to be seen along its long trek through the swamps is the small shipyard; although the yard is on its own, the nearest village being five miles down the road, we were informed nevertheless that it was technically within the city limits of New Orleans. When Jo heard this she didn't comment but looked skeptically at the sea of sawgrass rippling off into the wide blue yonder.

People ask, when you are traveling the Gulf Coast between New Orleans and Florida, whether you are following the Inland Waterway—as if there were any other way to go. For a small boat, an outboard cruiser, there isn't. There is a channel, marked and maintained by the ubiquitous Engineers and leading from the Mississippi Sound to Carrabelle in north Florida, but as an *inland* waterway it is a sometime thing. Many small-boat owners for whom "inland waterways" has connoted the sheltered sections of the Intracoastal Waterway on the Eastern Seaboard have had a rude awakening on the Gulf. Much of the channel there leads across open sea, although it may be called *X* Sound or *Y* Bay and appear on the chart to be landlocked between mainland and islands. The land is mostly out of sight and the waters are shallow, full of shelves and shoals that need very little wind to stir them up into a real mess. We had plenty of wind. It was *Sturm und Drang* for most of the way. The cold was intense, northerly winds nonstop from the Arctic, by the feel of them. Whenever we pulled into a boat dock at night the first thing we looked for was an outlet for the electric stove, which we could keep on all night to hold the twenty-degree temperature at bay. Every place we stopped Jo went shopping for more clothes. "Deep South," she'd mutter, struggling into yet another sweater.

Place names along the Mississippi-Alabama coasts are attractive. We dropped into Pass Christian (slightly on the Cornish side), for gas, but the Man with the Key (this again?) had gone fishing, so we went on to Biloxi, where we spent the night and were given a royal welcome and a bottle of orange wine with which to celebrate Thanksgiving ("Sort of harvest festival?" asked Jo innocently). Then at Pascagoula, tucked away up an overhung river in the boondocks (where they build submarines, of all things), the weather went from bad to gruesome, with a knife-edged wind and heavy rain creating abysmal misery.

I'd no grounds for complaint (which didn't stop me from complaining), because bad weather is an inevitable part of a long cruise, but Jo was by way of being an innocent bystander, and it seemed a long way for her to come to suffer. She didn't complain. She merely smiled bravely, looked trusting (why is it that brown eyes can always look so much more trusting than blue?) and retreated farther and farther into the folds of her increasingly voluminous garments. I felt like a cross between Legree and a con-man.

But before either one of us perished from misery or remorse we were rescued by a timely demonstration of that hospitality for which the American people are so rightly famed. Why the Marcussen family should have known about us is not clear—though it may be that two females at large in a boat are even more news-provoking than one, and there *had* been newspaper encounters on the way. Be that as it may, the Marcussens not only knew about us, they did something about us. They were boating people too, and had apparently said, in effect, "Those poor things," and driven twenty miles or so from their home to take us away from all that.

Warmth and the engaging demonstration that we had not after all been cast out into the snow did wonders to our circulations and morale, so that next morning we were ready to return to the fray. This desire was not wholly understood by our kind hosts, as the fray was still on the wild side, but obligingly they drove us back to the boat, stopping in town on the way for us to pick up such vital necessities as fuel for the stove (in the event of no electrical outlets) and more clothes for Jo.

Actually, we would not have left that day had it not been that time was running out faster than we were making headway, and we felt it imperative to at least make an effort to clock something on the log. Shortly we would have to be looking for a place in which to shelve the trip for a while, somewhere where it would be safe to leave *Gemini* and also from where it would be possible to return to Miami without either enormous expense or complications.

Getting to and from places slightly off the beaten track in the States is difficult, since personal transport seems to have been whittled down to travel by air or road. There are railways, but passenger traffic seems to run mainly between large centers, and the nearest station or halt, if you happen to be out in the sticks, may itself be a journey away. This situation also applies to air transport and, to a lesser extent, long-distance buses. Local buses are a rare and timid species, very hard to catch, requiring intimate knowledge of local conditions. If you haven't a car it is hard to get around. In this respect most of the northeast Gulf Coast could be regarded as being out in the sticks, and I reckoned we'd have to get at least to Florida for Miami-bound transportation.

So we departed, and as I have said, it was still on the wild side, though just how wild was not properly appreciated until we were out of the Pascagoula River and bounding about on the broken gray and whitecapped sea. Then we smartly lowered our sights from Dauphin Island, our intended destination, to Bayou LaBatre, twelve miles to the east'ard of Pascagoula, as the course thataway appeared to be slightly more sheltered. According to the chart it would seem that we would be in the lee of the land going to Bayou LaBatre. But in point of fact the water was too shoal for us — even for us — to get close enough to do us any good, and we had a rough run in slow time.

The river on which lies the fishing village of Bayou LaBatre is really quite lovely in a sylvan way, and to us it looked absolutely heavenly in the gathering dusk. We drove up and down between tree-walled banks, savoring the peace of it and casing the prospective parking places for a tie-up with a plug-in.

All the docks there were designed for large commercial fishing boats and were too tall for *Gemini*, who just about came to their knees. But we found a fishing camp which had a tiny boat basin, a skiff basin really, but more nearly our size, and there *Gemini* was ushered into a covered slip that was almost an exact fit.

There was an electrical outlet, praise be, over the catwalk at the end of the slip. We were completely protected from the weather and even from the wash of passing boats. The outlook for a quiet, comfortable night seemed promising.

About one o'clock in the morning I was roused by a curious *bonk-bonk* noise. It was vaguely familiar but it was some time before recognition filtered through the mists of sleep. The protest of too tight moorings on a falling tide. But that can't be, I said to myself from behind shuttered eyes, there aren't any tides here. Which, so far as I was concerned, disposed of the matter, and I tried to go back to sleep. But the *bonks* went on. Louder, increasingly insistent, refusing to be ignored. Jo murmured "S'at?" So at last, as with the dripping tap, the nudging door, the rattling window, I was bound to rise and deal with it, whatever it was.

The bowlines were bar taut, and the boat was all but hanging by her teeth. It didn't make sense because there are no tides in that area, but there was irrefutable evidence of an ebb right then, so I readjusted the lines and went back to bed without trying to figure out the reason. Whys could wait for the morning. It seemed that no sooner had I dropped off than the *bonks* began again and I had to get up and let out more line. This went on all night. In the morning there was little more than a skim of dew on the mud at the bottom of the boat basin, and *Gemini*'s bow was high and dry in the slip.

A fisherman was gloomily poling his skiff out of the basin. "Where'd the water go?" I asked him.

"Wind blew it away," he said.

"When will it come back?"

"When the wind changes."

Of course. I should have remembered. Strong winds have strong influences on the creeks, bays and inlets of non-tidal waters (they affect tidal waters too, but not with quite such devastating effect). A powerful offshore blow, *from* the land, sends the water galloping out to sea, and an onshore wind, one blowing *towards* the land, has it galloping back again. The strong northerlies we'd been having lately had pulled the plug and were fast draining the coastal areas. According to weather reports over the radio, the situation was likely to continue. The northerlies, it seemed, were not through. At present they were quiescent, but, one felt, thoughtfully licking their paws.

"Come on, Jo, let's get out of here before the water goes altogether."

With motors tilted we poled out of the basin with the boat hook.

Then in the safety of the deep waters of the river, we put the motors down and started them. The temperature was twenty degrees but the motors, being amenable machinery, obliged without protest.

"Where now?" asked Jo when we were clear of the river.

It was a good question. We had run from the mud, but ahead lay Mobile Bay, a dragon water about which we had heard nothing but warnings since New Orleans.

Separating Mississippi Sound from Mobile Bay is a causeway that runs across from the mainland to Dauphin Island. The channel passes through the causeway at a point near the island, and I thought that if the bay was acting up by the time we got there we could go in at Dauphin Island.

Which we did, because it was. Only to discover the Dauphin Island Marina was wide open to the wind then blowing and utterly useless to us as a refuge and a respite. We sidled down the island to look for something better and found a landlocked cove of sandy beaches, obviously destined to become waterfront lots in the near future but right then a splendid hideaway for us. We pulled the boat up on the steeply shelving beach, laid out the anchor, lit the stove and relaxed to wait for a better day.

All afternoon the wind blew furiously, but the sun came out and heartened us into taking a walk to the end of the island to see if the bay was as rough as the scudding clouds overhead indicated it should be. We were most gratified to find that it was. We also discovered that our cove was most conveniently sited within a few minutes walk of a shopping center where there was a marine as well as a grocery store.

Inadvertently we had found ourselves a perfect place to stop — natural solitude with the amenities right at hand. So I must say I was somewhat startled when Jo woke me with a cry of alarm next morning. But no wonder — she was standing on her head. Since it was my turn for sleeping the other way on I was standing on my feet, which wasn't nearly so disturbing. Looking out, we discovered *Gemini* hanging on her anchor line. The water had gone again, and the boat was pointing up at the sky.

"Oh dear," said Jo, facing the world from a normal angle again, "how unnerving not to be able to keep the sea under you."

We pushed the boat back into the water, glad of the steep slope, and wondered how long this draining business was going to go on.

For the time being, however, the winds appeared to have exhausted themselves. It turned out to be a superlative day and we made the most of it, once we got started. We raced across Mobile Bay, now all innocence, dimples and sparkles, and embarked, on the other side, on the portion of the Gulf Inland Waterway which is truly inland. It wasn't long before we crossed the Florida border — with loud cheers, as this marked a terrific advance. We finished our day's run at the excellent Sound Marina at Fort Walton Beach just in time to scamper across the road and watch the sun go down on the Gulf of Mexico in delicate shades of pink and green that spread all over the western sea and sky. "Like shot silk," said Jo.

"What a heavenly place to have sea like shot silk," she repeated as we crouched over supper in the cabin. But later I thought I detected a slight crack in her equanimity when she said as we crawled into our sleeping bags, "I wonder what it will be tonight."

The dockmaster had assured us that the water would stay put where *Gemini* was lying, so I said, "Rats, I expect."

But as a matter of fact, it was cats.

Thumpings in the cockpit, rustlings among the packages stowed overnight behind the windshield, paddings on the deck overhead woke us in the middle of the night.

"Rats," said Jo resignedly. "Huge American rats."

But it was cats all right, and next day we were buzzed by jets.

They came down out of nowhere as we were pounding along, eagerly piling up the miles, skimmed the boat top and zoomed off with a prodigious clap of thunder. The first time it happened, for a wild split second I thought the boat had unaccountably blown up.

After we'd cranked up our hearts again and spotted the culprits — small darts in the yonder — Jo merely commented that boating was certainly full of surprises.

We made a brief stop at Panama City, where the Joneses, who owned the attractive little Tarpon Docks at which we tied up for fuel, most kindly drove us about to shops and other necessary places of business such as banks and post offices. They even took us on a quick sight-seeing tour, of which I chiefly remember the gaunt skeletal structure of the piers and pilings of the vast new Municipal Docks.

The final day's dash in the afternoon took us through miles of cypress swamps, tall, untidy, fat-boled trees, gloomy with cobwebs of Spanish moss, to Apalachicola. There we groped in the dark through great rafts of water hyacinths to the Gulf Dock just as the men were putting out the lights and closing down for the night.

It was the first of December, and we had had two good days of weather. We could hardly hope for more, yet now we needed good conditions more than ever.

The Florida coast at Apalachicola turns sharply off in a northeasterly direction for about fifty miles to St. Marks, then turns in a southeasterly direction for approximately ninety miles to Cedar Key, where it repeats the dog-leg on a smaller scale. It was the first bight, the larger one, that was our immediate concern.

To go up to St. Marks, *north*ward again, and then down by the coast seemed a very long-winded, back-tracking way of tackling it, but the direct run across to Cedar Key meant a passage of over a hundred miles of open water, thirty miles offshore. Taking into consideration the time of year, and knowing how quickly Gulf waters can change from calm to calamitous, I wasn't wild about this prospect either. Between St. Marks and Cedar Key the coast is pretty barren of harbors, but there is a small fishing village, Steinhatchee, on a river, about half way along. By aiming for that, one could reduce the sea passage to sixty miles, but still be twenty miles or so off-shore. For a seventeen-foot outboard with seventy horse on the job, this could be a cinch, and over in two or three hours. In *good* weather. Bad weather is another story. Even the roundabout way by St. Marks was not easy, the whole of the coastal areas thereabouts being shoal and no place in which to be caught out. I wanted to be quite sure of the weather holding up before setting out for the crossing, whichever course I decided to take.

I called the weather bureau in the morning before it was light, only to get one of those ambiguous reports, no fault of the bureau, that leaves you where you went in. The dawn sky, which usually gives a fair idea of what's afoot for the day, was noncommittal that morning, but since the final decision did not have to be made just then we started out all the same.

The waterway at Apalachicola debouches into a large bay enclosed on the seaward side by long thin islands; the pass between two of the islands through which we would have to go to set a course for Steinhatchee, or Cedar Key or even St. Marks, lay several miles east of Apalachicola and just south of another fishing port, Carrabelle on the Crooked River.

I hoped that by the time we reached the pass the weather would be showing its true colors for the day. But no. It was fairly calm, but dark and lowering, ready to spring either way.

So we turned up towards Carrabelle, instead of out to sea.

We traced our way up the river to the gas docks and topped up the tanks: although we had hardly used any gas since they were filled the night before, I had decided on making for Steinhatchee, if we made for anywhere at all, and wanted to have every possible drop aboard for the crossing. I tried to get a more decisive weather report, with no more success than previously. It was calm now, but there was a front on the way, and who could say for sure when it would arrive? Meantime there would be light and variable winds. There might be ample time to get across. There might not. The portents were written plainly in the sky, but they didn't say when.

"Well, anyway, let's go out and have a look at it," said Jo gamely.

"Why not? We can always come back."

All the way down to the pass, five miles or so down the river and across the sound, I rode on the shall-we-shan't-we merry-go-round, but the beckoning beaches of Dog Island decided me: "Oh, hell, Jo, let's have some fun and go islanding instead."

Jo said, "You'd go, if you were on your own," but I wasn't having any of that, and was secretly enraged at myself for nearly falling into the dedication trap again. I hardly ever miss, being afflicted with a mail-must-go-through complex that makes me charge ahead on a project with undeviating fervor. This is all very well for me (though that is questionable) but certainly rough on those who, like Jo, may have got into the project by accident. For once, I managed to dump the mail bag in time, and we played hooky.

Dog Island turned out to be a very satisfactory desert island. There were no coconut palms, but it was several miles long and, so far as we knew, uninhabited, which made up for the lack of palms. Actually, as I was to discover with some surprise later, there is a ferry service to the other end of the island, but at our end there was no hint of this. The lovely long white beaches curved away into the distance to disappear round shallow inscrutable points; their only inhabitants seemed to be sea birds and soldier crabs. The island was very narrow where we were, and between the north and south shores there was a low jungle of scrub and thicket.

We anchored on the north side in shallow water and waded ashore. Then, as if the weather had been waiting for *us* to make up our minds, the sun came out, the lowering clouds settled themselves in tidy heaps on the horizon and it turned into an exquisitely clear, sparkling, blue-and-white day. A perfect day for traveling, but an even better one for islanding.

Wandering through the fierce spiny scrub we were set upon by weird cactus-type burrs, about the size of ping-pong balls, that clung to us with an animate tenacity. Jo swore they sprang at her from the bushes and wouldn't let go, and she wasn't inclined to think much of my assurance that they were flora rather than fauna. They looked like bright green sea urchins. Jo said, "I expect they're another of those fantastic American *things* that nobody else has ever thought of, and they probably *bark*."

I could see it was high time for my sister to see the country from a slightly less frenzied viewpoint.

We spent the afternoon beachcombing. It did not produce any great treasure, but ironed out the wrinkles in the nervous system and was altogether so pleasant we had half a mind to stay at the island overnight. But towards evening the clouds unrolled and spread across the sky and an authoritaive wind came bustling in from the north, so we upped anchor and drove back to Carrabelle, where we ran into the tall dock problem and finally had to settle for a berth in a lay-by out of town in the boondocks. We made fast by a bank to overhanging branches, astern of an aged oysterboat.

The north wind pulled the plug again, but we woke in the morning just in time to move the boat before she settled down on the razor blades of an oyster bed.

The weatherman on the radio reported small-craft warnings and thirty-mile-an-hour winds, and the low black clouds scudding overhead confirmed this. It was the day before we had planned to return to Miami anyway, so I reckoned at this point we could retire with honor, if transportation to Miami was reasonably available. It was, and arrangements were made to lay up the boat. We then departed to catch a bus to Tallahassee, from where we could in turn catch another bus to Miami, and once again the trip was left in abeyance. This time it took longer to get home by bus, although the distance was less, but it still felt like cheating.

11

"I'M SO glad your husband was with you for this bit. Now you've got the worst over and you'll be all right." The Captain looked earnestly at us across the table.

We had just completed a forty-mile shuttle with *Gemini* from Carrabelle to St. Marks, snatching a two-hour respite from an almost continuously bad weather report. Jo's departure for England was within a few days of Christmas and I had decided to stay home until then so that Bert could drive me back to Carrabelle over the long holiday weekend.

Oh dear, I thought at the Captain's remark, I mustn't let this bug me. He means well, and it *is* nice of him to be concerned, really, and he has been so kind, looking after *Gemini* and bringing the car round and all. So I twisted my face into a fatuous smile and said nothing, but Bert leapt on to a white horse and gallantly waved a lance. "I don't see why you should get so excited about this little stretch of water," said he, "it's nothing to her. She sailed across the Atlantic alone."

"Maybe," said the Captain, "but these are very treacherous waters. I've sailed them all my life, and I'll admit I treat them with every respect. Many a time I . . . She *what* . . . ?"

He swung round and studied me with as much amazement and incredulity as if Bert had said I really had four arms and two of them were hidden under my coat. He asked some very mollifying questions about the ocean crossing, and then added with a twinkle in his eye: "I still say you've got the worst over and that it'll be easy from now on, and I'm still glad you weren't alone for this bit."

In Carrabelle it hadn't been easy to find a place in which to leave *Gemini*. All the docks there were too high and too open for her. But finally after Jo and I had searched the waterfront, testing every quay for size and security, and had cross-examined nearly everyone on them, we tracked down a new boat basin being excavated, almost out of the solid, adjacent to a motel. The basin was still in a state of nature, a large muddy pool, but there was plenty of water in it, it was beautifully protected from all winds and wakes, and it was right under the eye of the management.

The management was a most accommodating couple, and after the situation had been explained to them, they called up the Captain, who owned the motel and various other thriving enterprises in town. He gave his blessing and in short order *Gemini* was ensconced in the environs of the earthworks.

They are not pikers in Carrabelle. They get things done. The boat basin was in operation two weeks later when I returned with Bert, at midnight on Christmas Eve. *Gemini* had been moved to a berth under our motel window, where she awaited us, fendered against the new quay wall.

We had decided to do what shuttling we could over the holiday; all projects must come to an end and it was time to wind this one up. But Christmas Day was a brute for traveling so we ambled up the wooded reaches of the Crooked River for a picnic instead.

By then I had given up the idea of a direct crossing to Steinhatchee. Any mention of so doing sent local fishermen and party-boat captains into an attack of the fits and gibbers; the chances of good conditions for such a crossing occurring for long enough, soon enough and definitely enough were growing less and less with each day of winter's advance.

Reluctant to separate for even a moment of our short time together, we asked the Captain about bus services between St. Marks and Carrabelle. He said there weren't any, but added, "I'll tell you what — you call me when you get to St. Marks, and I'll bring your car round for you."

St. Marks, six miles from the sea or thereabouts, lies on a winding river that is itself an offshoot of another, the Wakulla. The St. Marks River is narrow and flanked by thick stands of shaggy trees and leggity pom-pom palms. The town appears to consist of two restaurants, a small store, a permanently occupied phone booth, a motor court, no dwellings visible to the naked eye, and a plethora of docks, ship- and boatyards. We tied up at one, a combination gas dock and party-boat concern, where Bert reduced the owner, Curtis Shields, to hysterics by announcing his intention of leaving me in the morning. "Hey, Myrt," Shields shouted to his wife, "he says he's going to leave her to look after herself in the boat. How d'ya like that, huh?"

In the morning when he found Bert had really gone he said, "By God, he said he would!"

As arranged, we phoned the Captain from St. Marks, and agreed to meet him at one of the restaurants. We intended, after we had had dinner together, to drive him back to Carrabelle, but when he arrived we found he'd kindly saved us this journey by having a friend follow him in his (the Captain's) car.

In the restaurant Bert said, "How about a drink?" The Captain said *hmph*, looked right and left, jerked his head towards the door, and said out of the corner of his mouth, "Come on outside." A man once sidled up to me in a West Indian village street and muttered, "How about a bottle of Blind Tiger?" It was rather like that. We followed him out to his car where he fumbled about in the back in the dark to produce a clinking bundle. "Crowd round," directed the Captain, and the bundle, a bottle and jigger glass masked under a cloth, was passed round surreptitiously. So there we were in this space age clustered together sneaking drinks like a bunch of adolescents sneaking smokes, as guilty a looking lot as ever plotted the downfall of a dictator.

"I thought Prohibition was repealed?"

"Not here, it wasn't. Florida is an optional state. This is a dry county."

Bert left for Miami at first light in the morning and I considered the next step on the way. Quite a long step it was, ninety miles to Cedar Key. A study of the chart showed that shoals ran out from the shore for several miles; the few places one might go in in an emergency were over the halfway mark and so far off course that one might just as well aim to make the trip in one. That day the weather report was bad, so I spent it uncluttering the boat. Next morning was worse, so I spent it on a fishing trip up the river. The morning after that the weather looked noncommittal and I phoned the weather bureau, explaining where I wanted to go and in what kind of boat I was going, to see if there was the slightest chance of my ever being able to do it. Not today, I was told. Northwest winds, twenty-five miles an hour. "But they should diminish by tonight," said the weatherman, "and tomorrow conditions should be just right for you. There's nothing in sight that says otherwise."

Fortunately I was beguiled by the still, sunny morning into disregarding his advice and setting out, for just as I got into the Wakulla River, a mile or so from the sea, the starboard motor quit.

Not gas. Not plugs. I drove back to Curtis Shields's dock on the port motor, thankful that there was a port motor to drive back on, that it had happened before the good traveling day was due to arrive, and that it hadn't happened at sea. If the motor had wanted to break down, it couldn't have been more cooperative about it.

The nearest Evinrude dealer was at Tallahassee, twenty miles away. Curtis took the motor off and loaded it into his truck and Myrtle drove it into town with me perched up in the cab beside her.

The repair shops at the outboard dealer's were humming. There were motors in every state of deshabille waiting their turn and it didn't look as though there was a hope in weeks of getting mine fixed. Desperately I explained how it was and how tomorrow was supposed to be a good day and who knew when — or if — it would happen again this winter. Willett Hancock looked up from the job he was doing and said to a man standing by: "You hear that? What do you say?" and the man said, "Sure. I'm not in that much of a hurry."

Whilst the motor underwent hospitalization — for a recalcitrant water pump, as it turned out — Myrtle gave me a truck tour of the town, including a turn round the Florida State University's splendid grounds. The drive convinced me that it is about time the car manufacturers got us back to being tall in the saddle again.

Tallahassee has a fine country-town dignity as befits its condition as state capital. It is built on rolling hills and the streets are studded with trees. I have a picture in my mind of white buildings as seen through a tracery of twigs and branches. The architecture is neither aggressively modern nor quaintly antiquated and the effect is very restful. It is the only town I have seen where the usual process of town encroaching on countryside has been reversed. Here the country encroaches on the town. On all counts I was charmed by Tallahassee.

All afternoon it was gratifying to observe the clouds belting overhead on a nor'wester — just like the man said. By evening it was diminishing, and the motor was ready.

As both motors inevitably underwent the same conditions, it seemed reasonable to suppose that whatever had caused one water pump to go out of whack might similarly have affected the other. A test made on our return proved this to be the case. It was too late then to hotfoot back to Tallahassee, but early next morning we gave an encore to the previous day's performance with Curtis removing the motor and Myrtle driving it to town, and Willett Hancock patiently shelving his amenable customers. The net result was that at half past eleven I was steaming down the river on my way to Cedar Key, and keeping a lookout for platforms.

These are an unusual feature of the marinescape hereabouts. They look like giant tables, which is what they are, giant bird tables for the collection of guano. Sited at irregular intervals round the coast, they are shown on the chart as small squares and would seem to be a useful adjunct to navigation. I often heard boatmen on the Mississippi, Florida-bound, discussing the advisability of "following the platforms," but it is not advisable at all, because the position of the platforms as shown on the chart ain't necessarily so. They are frequently out of place, nonexistent, or standing in a few inches of water, and are fascinatingly incongruous to encounter out of sight of land in what appears to be open sea.

The weatherman's forecast came true and it was a spanking run to Cedar Key — in more ways than one. For although there was only a light breeze the sea was lumpy and I could see it would have to be reckoned with in a wind with any force behind it.

At the end of the run I tied up at a dock that was too tall and somewhat rickety, but it was growing dark and there was no choice. All the docks in this part of the world were built for big boats, shrimpers and drifters and trawlers and big yachts. Small boats were auxiliaries and didn't need docks for themselves. By standing on the cockpit coaming I could just see across the pier.

An elderly man, slight and neatly dressed, stepped carefully to the edge of the dock with the fuel hose filler in his hand. This he thrust out horizontally from him, far above my head, but where I would be on the type of cruiser for which the dock catered. I realized he was blind.

"Thank you," I said, "but this is an outboard cruiser and I'll have to put the oil in first."

But he went on offering the hose and I went on trying to explain, when suddenly in a dawning mixture of horror and compunction I realized he was deaf as well as blind.

His wife appeared anxiously from a building and rescued us both. "He won't give up," she said, gently leading him away. "We've tried to get him away from here, but it has been his life. . . . I'll send a boy to help you."

Gemini woke me in the morning nudging against the pilings. A brisk wind was making up and it was clearly time to get moving, for there was little shelter where I was. The weather report was discouraging as usual, and the general appearance of the dawn did nothing to dispute it; but there was nothing for it but to move along down the coast.

At Cedar Key the Florida coast takes off on another

excursion eastward, but only for ten miles this time, to the Waccasassa River, where it turns south again. The bay so enclosed is shallow with soundings of up to five feet only and it is bestrewn with oyster bars. There was nothing to be gained by going into or anywhere near the Waccasassa River, so I set a course for a light marking the outer entrance to the Withlacoochee River (Hiawatha country, for sure. Just hear that Minnehaha. And a pox upon the purists who would have the Hiawatha country somewhere else). I thought that if the weather picked up I could always go on and go into any of the several inlets farther south, and if it did not, then there was always the Withlacoochee.

It was only twelve miles to the light, but it was the roughest run of the trip, not excluding some of the darker moments in the North Channel.

The sea boiled. It built up into horrid pyramids and tumbled all ways in a welter of foam. *Gemini* would drop off the edge of a wave-cliff and stop dead in the bottom of a trough, deluged under a solid wall of water. It was blowing quite hard, but not enough to justify the roughness of the seas, which were making a hurricane out of a twenty-mile wind. I imagined that the configuration of the sea bed, the numerous river outflows and the various currents must account for it, and that I might possibly do better farther out to see. But I didn't know that I would for sure. I was already ten miles off shore, and with conditions undeniably deteriorating, did not wish to diminish the chances of going in if it should become necessary to do so.

I stayed on course for the Withlacoochee light, gradually closing the land, and in due course a light appeared, bobbing up momentarily between wave tops.

It was on the starboard hand — on the right-hand side of the boat — and ahead. The channel leading through the shoals to the entrance to the Withlacoochee River is about five miles long, and there are two lights in it. One marks the outermost limits of the channel, where the water round about is nine feet deep, and the other is about a mile and a half farther in, at the beginning of the channel proper, where soundings are a foot or less.

Even with binoculars it was impossible to distinguish the light. It flashed into view now and then and one only knew from experience that it was a light at all. If it was the outer light, all was well, but if it was the inner light I was heading for a mess of trouble.

Gingerly I advanced, keeping a wary eye out all round, as is my habit. Then suddenly, about three quarters of a mile abeam on the starboard side, out to sea, it was breaking white on a small brown island.

And there wasn't any land on that side of me for a thousand miles. If that was land then, I was way off course to the left, in amongst the shoals for sure, and could expect to grind up in the maelstrom any minute.

There are few sensations as devastating as the disorientation a navigator feels when land turns up where it shouldn't. The bottom has completely dropped out of his world. He is weightless, witless, and zooming about in outer space without a capsule.

It is not easy to run an exact compass course in an

outboard in rough weather. The card spins like a top. But I've been following compasses for more than twenty years and have a fair notion of what's going on. I didn't think I could have got *that* far off. Still . . . The light at this stage meant nothing. An object had appeared in the place where a light was expected to appear, at the time when it was expected to appear, and I jumped to the conclusion it was the light. Now that this wretched little island had come up I didn't know what it might be.

Meantime, what to do? When in doubt, I thought, sailboat tactics. Out to sea with you, my lass.

So I inched seaward, wondering what was underneath, expecting to hit any moment, and I kept a watch on the alien intruding island.

As its bearing altered, it seemed that its general aspect did too. And were my eyes funny, or was it heaving just a little???

I shifted into neutral and whilst the boat wallowed with the comical quick wag of her kind I had a painstaking session with the binoculars.

And did not believe what I thought I saw even after ten minutes juggling with the glasses, not until I had moved in a lot closer and made sure.

The "island" was a barge, a big old Mississippi oil barge, laden and awash, untended and lying at anchor eight miles out. Dropped off by a tow, no doubt, and waiting to be picked up by a tug for local delivery.

Bird tables and barges — what next in Jo's shot-silk sea? Huffed but lighter-hearted I turned back for the light, which *was* a light and the right one.

There is no margin for error in the channel that leads

from the light to the Withlacoochee River. The tight little passage winds over the shoals with jagged rocks awash beside the markers, which fortunately are as thick as a picket fence, and which incidentally are the only signs of the hand of man thereabouts. If it wasn't for the markers on the journey upstream one would wonder if by some wild chance the place had been overlooked and one was the first there. There are no subdivisions, trailer parks, boat docks, filling stations, ice cream parlors, billboards or beer cans to show either Columbus or Kilroy had been that way. And although it is on the 29th parallel, which is pretty far north, tropically speaking, the Withlacoochee has the voluptuous overladen appearance of a tropical river: heavy foliage drooping into the water, tall inquiring palms, a listening stillness that gives one the feeling of being watched by thousands of invisible eyes. For a few miles nothing would surprise you on the Withlacoochee, from a pterodactyl to a tiger. Then you come to Yankeetown and another illusion bites the dust. Not that Yankeetown isn't a perfectly delightful place, I must hasten to add, but it is a habitation and means you aren't the first.

I tied up at the Riverside Fishing Camp where *Gemini* towered over the skiffs and probably got delusions of grandeur from being the big boat in port. As soon as I opened my mouth one of the brothers who owned the camp said, "You sound like a limey." Oddly enough he was one of the few to recognize the accent. Generally, whilst it was realized that it was different, most people thought I was Swedish or Norwegian, often German or Dutch, and the closest they got to home was

Scotland. This was particularly marked in the Middle West—where it would appear no Englishman has set foot! When I told the camp owner that I *was* a limey, he said, "Then you must be lost. No one comes up here unless they're lost."

It being New Year's Eve and the brink of another holiday weekend, I called Bert immediately on arrival. He arrived at midnight with the fly rods, saying enthusiastically, "Wonderful bass-fishing waters here," but New Year's Day was a stinker and literally washed that idea out. Towards evening it cleared up, and the camp owner, who along with his brother was an import from the North and as charmed with the locale as any visitor, insisted on taking us for a boat ride to the island-spattered coast. We went in one of his flat-bottomed skiffs, because where we were going was too shallow for *Gemini*. Indeed, the coastal waters round the Withlacoochee area seemed to be only inches deep. Knowing them intimately, our pilot drove at a rate of knots, threading his way confidently through the islands, skipping across oyster beds and flipping the outboard motor. It was twilight and the innumerable islands, compact desert isles, complete with humpbacked jungle and long-stemmed palms, stood silhouetted against the glowing, rain-washed sky.

It was so obviously worthy of exploration that we regretted the following day being so good for traveling. But good traveling days cannot be wasted in winter, and we made a run down to Venice that day which has become such a standard passage that all others are compared to it—"this is as good as that run to Venice"

— or "not such good weather as we had on the Venice trip." We only stopped at Venice because the car was then 120 miles behind us and Bert had to get it back in order to return to Miami the following night. The farther we went the more complicated the shuttle service became. As it was, we regained the car comparatively easily with two bus hops and a hitchhike.

When Bert dropped me off at the boat again, he said confidently, "You'll be home in a couple of days," and continued on his way to Miami. Our parting was cheerful for the first time.

All that remained of the Grand Tour was a final scamper down the Gulf to Boca Grande, where the breakers were impressive even though they didn't mean anything that day. This was followed by a sheltered ride through the islands, Pine and Sanibel of shell fame, to Fort Myers, where I stopped at the lordly, balustraded yacht basin for a cross-state chart. After which came some hand-to-hand fighting with the water hyacinth that all but choked the Caloosahatchee River up to La Belle, where I stopped for the night at the picturesque but decrepit town wharf. I tried to call Bert, only to find the town's entire phone system out of order ("Likely story," growled my husband, after communications had been restored at 11 P.M.).

In the morning there were three more locks to be negotiated, kid stuff after the Illinois giants. The lock at Moore Haven had an interesting side-effect in a boat basin I visited there to refuel. It raised and lowered the water level as it operated and kept the boats in the basin going up and down on a seemingly perpetual elevator ride.

On the other side of the lock at Moore Haven lay Okeechobee, the largest fresh-water lake entirely within U.S. mainland borders — and the point on the journey that meant I was "home." Lake Okeechobee is one of our favorite fishing grounds; Bert and I have spent many a weekend there trying to outwit the bass. I saluted our favorite spots in passing, regretting it was necessary to pass, and I marveled, as usual, at the lake's impressive light structure near Clewiston that has so many meteorological measuring devices whirring and turning on it that it looks like a colossal mobile. Then I crossed Okeechobee to embark on an unexpectedly choppy run along the St. Lucie Canal and River. However, it was not choppy enough to delay progress, and it seemed no time before I was skirting the town of Stuart once more and heading southward down the Intracoastal Waterway.

It was six months since I had passed that way at the beginning of the journey, and I was startled to find that the Waterway was almost unrecognizable with the new developments that had sprung up on either side. I would have thought that saturation point in housing had been reached long ago, and that the erection of even the most meager kennel on the waterfront would have been pretty well impossible. A foolish thought. One thing I might have learned is that few Americans readily recognize the meaning of the word "impossible." Bert was at Dinner Key to meet me, and Steve, dapper in his city-suit disguise as a newspaperman. Roncallo bustled down to the quay, aggrieved and shrugging: "You never told us you were coming back today — no one knows — no one's here to meet you . . ."

I thought, Bert's here, who else matters?

Time went into reverse as *Gemini* was put into slings and hoisted ashore. Automatically, Bert, Steve and I moved over to her as she hung suspended prior to being lowered on to a trailer, and we stroked her hull as one runs a hand down the legs of a horse after a race.

"No dents?" said Steve in a tone of surprise.

"Whaddaya mean, no dents?" I said truculently.

Bert grinned, "That's my gal. Spoken like a native."

CPSIA information can be obtained
at www.ICGtesting.com
Printed in the USA
LVHW051400300623
751029LV00007B/1124

9 781014 912305